NETWORK LIKE A MILLIONAIRE

PRACTICAL STRATEGIES FOR INCREASING
YOUR NET WORTH WITH SOCIAL CAPITAL

MICHAEL WILSON

ISBN 978-1-66786-964-3

TABLE OF CONTENTS

THANK YOU

· · · · · · · · · · · · · · · · · · · ·

This book could not be possible without the inspiration of my wife, Cristina Wilson. She encouraged and motivated me to write this book.

I also want to thank my children, Michelle and Christian, and my parents, James and Neomi Sigler, for cheering me on.

Thank you, Dr. RL Chance, who guided me on how to write this book.

Thank you, Rich Gomez, for the resources and inspiration.

FOREWORD

You'll hear the saying "Your network is your net worth" until the day you die - It's something that all great business owners and entrepreneurs know to be true, but only some try to live it.

The problem is that most people don't get further than the saying. Most people stop right there. Maybe they attend all the networking events they're supposed to, say all the right things, and even occasionally get some business out of it, maybe. This might help them short term, but it doesn't build any long-term value. There are very few people that I have met who fully understand this.

As the President of Network Lead Exchange, one of the fastest-growing business networking groups in the world, I see many people trying to network for all the wrong reasons. I also get the pleasure of meeting many people who do it for all the right reasons. Michael Wilson is one of those guys. From the first conversation I had with Michael, he was asking me questions and trying to genuinely understand my company and me. We share a similar vision of networking and, what Michael calls it in this book, social capital. Michael is a living, breathing example of servant leadership. He's a military veteran, volunteer, business coach, mentor, and much more. I am proud and honored to also call him a friend.

> Austin Titus
> President
> Network Lead Exchange

INTRODUCTION

·····························

"You can have everything in life you want if you will just help enough other people get what they want."—Zig Ziglar

The net worth of the richest man in the world, Elon Musk is around $273,000,000,000 (Forbes 2022). According to the Forbes World Billionaires List 2022, there are a total of 2,668 billionaires globally. What comes to mind when you think about these affluent individuals? Most of us feel inspired, some aspire to emulate their success stories in their own lives, a few of us like to read about their expensive possessions and luxurious lifestyles, and a handful tries to discover the possible reasons behind their unparalleled accomplishments. What is your opinion about the secret to their success?

Running a business isn't easy by any stretch of the imagination and carrying it to the pinnacle of success requires hard work and perseverance. Take a look at any Fortune 500 company and you will find a great business idea behind its high stock price and a bunch of brilliant minds maneuvering every day to achieve those attractive revenue figures. There will most likely be an out-of-the-box product or service out in the market making life easy for a large number of people or solving a problem in the best way yet. When Apple introduced the iPod, it was the slimmest electronic audio and video device providing easy access to thousands of songs right from your pocket. When the Inditex group launched Zara, it was one of the first companies to introduce a new collection of stylish apparel in its stores every fortnight. When Facebook entered the scene in 2004, social media was an unknown term in many parts of the world, and making connections with people from a country other than your own was still difficult.

Success in business doesn't have to be only about the Fortune 500 or Forbes Rich list. Look around in your local community, and you will find entrepreneurial ventures that are nascent but poised for exponential growth and success. The number of zeros in the profit numbers of most megacorps have their origin in their seedling days. So what are these businesses doing right? What is it that separates these star entrepreneurs from the ordinary ones? Is it just the business idea or something beyond that?

If you look closely at any business, you will find that there are people involved every step of the way. An entrepreneur is never the only person behind a business even if what they're running is a sole proprietorship. No one is skilled enough to perform every activity of their business on their own. If you have an innovative business idea, you will need someone to make it tangible for you. If you are a techno-wizard, you will most likely require assistance with administration and management. You will need qualified professionals to help you with the legal and compliance aspects of your venture. Getting a bank loan or investor onboard, striking a deal with a collaborator, creating a distribution channel for your product, marketing your offering and every other activity you undertake to generate income from your business will require you to connect with people at different levels. Opportunities come through people. Finding solutions to problems requires the involvement of people. Knowing the right people at the right time can do wonders for your business in ways you cannot imagine. As a business owner, you will require financial capital to get your business off the ground, run and grow it, and acquire resources. You will need human capital to bring value to your organization and manage its affairs. There is, however, another kind of capital that is the key to entrepreneurial success, and that is called the "social capital". This form of capital is so powerful that it can help you build and acquire every kind of capital and resource you will possibly need for your business. Whether you are earning in the millions or have just started out, having a network of supporters is essential to sail through the bumpy road of entrepreneurship with ease.

I started my journey as a business coach back in 2014, mainly coaching small to midsize businesses. My job exposed me to all kinds of entrepreneurs and provided me with a good understanding of what drives them. Through this journey, I learned that all entrepreneurs are characteristically the same kind of people. No matter what kind of business they are in, they are inherent risk-takers and share the same grit, determination, and passion for their business. One clear pattern that came to light over these years was that most of them had little to no knowledge or understanding of the importance of building their network. Creating a network is one of the key ingredients to success, one which self-made millionaires throughout history have been using to build their empires. Social capital is as valuable as financial and human capital can give rise to relationships that can contribute to the growth of your business in a myriad of different ways.

This book will shed light on the concept of social capital and will take you through the steps you can follow to use this goldmine to your advantage. As you flip through these pages, you will learn:

- What is the business silo of self-employment?

- What are the three kinds of capital?

- What is social capital, and how building your social capital will benefit you?

- How to go about building your network?

- What is the power of relationships and how do you maintain them?

- What are those common mistakes people tend to make while building their social capital, and what are those steps you can take to avoid them?

- What is a business alliance and how can it help you?

It's easy to get lost among all these questions and feel overwhelmed by them all. This is why so many would-be entrepreneurs silently give up on the fight to become the best they could be and return to the cat and mouse game of the corporate grind. But it doesn't have to be that way.

Sowing the seed of entrepreneurship and toiling hard to make it blossom into something beautiful and inspirational is no less than a thrilling adventure. As dreamy and fulfilling as it might seem, this experience can also be isolating at times. There are sure to be a lot of whys and how-tos you will need answers to along the way. Invest your time and effort in building your social capital today, and you will never feel alone. Come on, let's create a strong foundation together on which you can build a majestic business empire of your own. The master key to the door of entrepreneurial success is just here. Are you ready to grab it and step in?

CHAPTER ONE:

....

SOCIAL CAPITAL, WHAT IS IT?

When we think of the word "capital", most of us associate it with money. Capital, however, is much more than the financial angle of a business we tend to couple it with. The dictionary will provide you with a host of different meanings for the word. In business, the term capital can mean three different things. These three meanings come from the different areas of a business, i.e., finance, human resources, and public relations. Let's look at all of these in turn.

FINANCIAL CAPITAL

Finance is considered the lifeblood of a business. Financial capital is a resource that is measured in terms of money and is used by entrepreneurs to make and sell their products or provide their services to their customers. Anything that can be expressed in monetary terms can be accounted for as financial capital. This form of capital can also include machinery, tools, factory, and land used to operate the business. It is almost impossible to start and run an enterprise without money, and this is true for most businesses in the world. The amount of money required by a business might vary in accordance with its nature: for example, setting up a manufacturing unit is more capital intensive when compared to establishing a corner shop on your street or starting a baking business from home. The stage at which you will require the funds may be different for different types of businesses. For instance, a talent-based business will require more money for marketing, a service business will not require much money at the start, and a fashion label will require money at all stages from setting up shop to producing the inventory to distribution and marketing. The source of the capital might also vary from business to business and entrepreneur to entrepreneur. There are so many different ways in which the money required for a business can be raised. The source of funds can be broadly categorized as internal or external. Internal funding comes from the entrepreneur themselves. You might have enough savings to start your business, you might choose to borrow funds from your friends and family members, or you might decide to sell an asset or a valuable personal belonging. Whatever the manner, the entrepreneur makes their own arrangements by making use of their inner circle.

The second option is adopted by those entrepreneurs who require a sum of money that is too large to be collected through internal sources. Some business owners also choose to adopt the external method of raising funds when all of their efforts with the internal method have been unsuccessful. As the name suggests, this method involves approaching people and organizations outside one's inner circle for investment. One option is to go to a bank for a loan. Many banks out there have funding programs for new entrepreneurs as well as mature enterprises. Approaching high-net-worth individuals, venture capitalists, or angel investors is another very popular way of securing funding for a business. While banks primarily only provide the capital required for the business, this second category of people and organizations can help entrepreneurs in the day-to-day functioning of the business and provide advice when required aside from buying a piece of the organization through their financial contribution. Both of these above-discussed methods of securing external funding can help an entrepreneur to raise any amount of money and are popularly used in the corporate world, but some business owners find these methods complicated and time-consuming because of the stringent formalities and paperwork associated with them.

Putting it all together, the amount raised by an entrepreneur for his venture could either be debt or equity. When the person or organization providing the capital is offered a share in the ownership of the business, such capital is called equity capital. Funds brought on board through friends and family members, personal savings, and angel investors are some examples of equity capital. Money raised in this way isn't a loan and doesn't have to be returned. A certain rate of return, say 5% of the sum contributed, is paid to the owners of the capital annually in the form of a dividend. This, however, isn't mandatory and is at the discretion of the entrepreneur. Those holding ownership in a business by way of their financial contribution are free to sell their stake to someone else if they wish to recover their dues. Debt capital, on the other hand, is a borrowed sum of money that has to be repaid to its owner. A bank loan is a classic example of debt capital. Sometimes, family members and other people contributing money in their personal capacity might also opt to do so in the form of debt instead of equity. Debt capital does not dilute the ownership of the business allowing the entrepreneur to have complete control. The person or organization contributing money in the form of debt is not entitled to any proportional share in the ownership of the business. Such financiers are compensated by way of periodic interest payments. Debt capital is much riskier than equity capital, and those businesses that are unable to repay their creditors may even have to file for bankruptcy.

When people use the word "capital," they almost always are exclusively referring to "financial capital." Broadly speaking, capital is actually a resource. It is a means to create value and profits for a business. While it cannot be denied that money is essential to carry out business activities and eventually generate revenue for an organization, can a high-tech office building, a massive piece of land, or a bank account full of money start, run, and grow a business on its own? Never in a million years. Even the most novel business idea in the world can get nowhere without the involvement of a human brain. Financial capital is definitely important for a business but it most certainly isn't the only ingredient for success. Financial capital only has value when it is in the hands of a human being, and this brings us to the second kind of capital without which no business activity is possible.

HUMAN CAPITAL

This is an invaluable intangible asset that cannot be listed on the balance sheet of a company but is crucial for its existence, growth, and success. Human capital refers to the economic value of a worker's experience and skills (Kenton 2022). It includes assets such as employee education and training, intelligence, experience, all kinds of management skills and other employee attributes, loyalty, punctuality, and other qualities that employers value. It is an investment of a company in its employees.

An organization is considered only as good as the people working in it. It is people who run and grow an organization. Every person working at a company is a mix of different qualities and characteristics. All of these varied personalities come together to shape the personality of an organization. While it's true that the personality of the person in the top seat has a greater influence on an organization, every single employee has a role to play. The concept of human capital advocates that no worker is equal, but the quality of employees can be improved by investing in them. So what does it mean to invest in human capital?

Simply put, an investment in human capital for a business owner would entail conducting employee training and development programs. This can include sponsoring the higher education of employees, designing workshops to help employees improve their skills such as managing time, coping with stress in the workplace, dealing with difficult work situations and clients, and working in teams both large and small. The employee training and development program of some businesses also includes career planning for their staff. Specialized sessions are also held to teach employees different methods and techniques to improve their efficiency and performance in their jobs. They are given lessons to help sharpen and enhance their problem-solving skills, communication skills, technical skills, creativity, resilience, emotional intelligence, and mental health. On several occasions, the workforce of a business comprises people from different religious, geographical, and cultural backgrounds. To ensure a productive and harmonious work environment, providing such employees with adequate training sessions and lectures on teamwork is crucial for a business. This is especially true for large and growing companies, and for those businesses that are located in cosmopolitan cities.

We all know PepsiCo Inc, the Fortune 500 megacorporation headquartered in the US that makes snacks and beverages. Like most other large companies in the world, this one too has its own human resource management (HRM) policies in place to build its human capital. At PepsiCo, the belief is that people are their greatest assets. Its HR department focuses on people development, and in order to do that, systems are put in place to encourage employees to work to their full potential. A collaborative and mutually supportive work environment is created at all their offices around the globe to encourage people to grow and flourish. Performance management and reward systems are developed to motivate the workforce to keep working hard. Thorough training is provided to all employees right at the start of their employment. Employees are provided with leadership development sessions, career development planning programs, and one on one sessions with qualified professionals to solve their problems. Steps are taken to ensure the overall well-being of all employees and to provide them with direction in life. Relationship building is the key focus of the human resource department at PepsiCo. Policies and rules are put in place to create a flexible, friendly, and conversant business environment to enhance employee performance and bring the best out of them. Regular performance evaluation and assessment are carried out to ensure that the right people are at the right place within the organization, and continual efforts are taken to foster learning and improve efficiency.

Human capital has been proven to increase the productivity and profitability of an enterprise. The more an organization invests in its human resources, the greater its chances of success. An increase in human capital is known to bring about innovation and growth. As discussed above in the PepsiCo example, the HR department of a company is in charge of managing and developing its human capital. The idea and concept of human capital isn't a recent one. It has been around since the 18th century when Adam Smith spoke about its benefits in his book, *An Inquiry into the Nature and Causes of the Wealth of Nations.* So what's the bottom line? The importance and benefits of investing in human capital cannot be emphasized enough.

There is, however, another angle to the human resource management policies of companies, and this involves recruiting the right kind of people; the
ones that have in them the potential and open-mindedness to be molded
into something extraordinary. It is true that an investment in human capital can help a great deal in developing employees, but as the famous saying
goes, "You can lead a horse to water, but you can't make it drink." So, what
does this mean? You might have an adequate supply of funds to invest in
your human capital, and the most intelligent people to impart knowledge
and provide training to your staff, but you as a business owner can only shape
and train who you have access to. You can definitely make use of the many
recruitment services available out there to hire employees, but the most
appropriate and the highest quality people are often found only with the help
of connections. Having the right kind of canvas to play around with is very
important to create a masterpiece, and this can be accomplished if you have
the right connections to help you bring good talent onboard. Connections
mean a network of people you know; a group of people who can help you
with everything you might require in the course of managing and operating
your business. So, where in the world do you get these connections from?
The answer to this lies in the next section in which we will discuss a resource
that is the secret to every millionaire's success: social capital.

SOCIAL CAPITAL

This is the most vital, yet the most neglected form of capital in the business
world. We, humans, are social beings longing for connection with people.
Maslow's Hierarchy of Needs, a popular theory in the social sciences that lists
the universal needs of human beings, also mentions social connections. As
per the theory, the most important needs of humans are the most basic physiological and safety needs like food, clothing, shelter, and a safe environment
for existence and health. Soon after these basic needs are met, all human
beings need social connections for survival. There are plenty of theories in
the sciences that emphasize the importance and benefits of networking, but
most business owners tend to ignore it. So, what exactly is social capital?

Different authors have provided different definitions for the term social capital, but there is one theme that is prevalent in most of them. Social capital is the outcome of social relationships. Social capital is a collection of your social assets. It is a measure of the value of the network of relationships that a person has built over their lifetime. These social links and bonds can be a result of a friendship group, or can also spring from your daily interactions with people. Having a conversation with a friend's friend, speaking to someone seated next to you on the train, the relationships you build with the people you meet as you go about your day at work, every new colleague or client you talk to, and every interaction you have with someone outside of your inner circle of family members and friends contributes to your social capital. The concept of social capital revolves around the belief that these networks and relationships have the potential to provide a multitude of benefits and solutions to people's problems. Having social capital means having the knowledge or ability to call on the right person to help in a certain situation.

Human beings have been harnessing the power of relationships for generations, but the term social capital has come into popular usage only since the 1990s. The concept however has been intermittently used for a much longer time. In the words of famous theorist L.J. Hanifan, "If one man may come into contact with his neighbors, and they with other neighbors and so on, this would lead to the accumulation of social capital". To put it in simple terms, social capital is an investment in social relationships. These relationships could be with your neighbors, with people in your locality, in social groups consisting of people from different parts of the country you live in, or even in organizations involving the participation of people from across borders. French sociologist Pierre Bordieu suggests that the wealthy and powerful use social capital to maintain advantages for themselves in society.

For an entrepreneur trying to establish and expand their venture, social capital is no less than a goldmine. Meeting people and building relationships should necessarily be a part of every business owner's weekly schedule. With the introduction of social media, networking for business has become so much easier. Before social media, people had to make long, uncomfortable journeys to meet someone or attend a networking event. Now, building relationships can easily be done online from the comfort of your own home with the click of a button. The relationships you will build through your social capital can help in the more efficient production of your goods and services. It can literally make or break a business. The social capital of a business owner needn't always consist of colleagues, suppliers, co-workers, and other stakeholders. Knowing other business owners and as many people as possible in your particular business field will definitely be helpful, but building relationships with a wide variety of people from different backgrounds and professions at a personal level is like an investment whose value we don't realize until we see or experience the gain.

TYPES OF SOCIAL CAPITAL

When we interact with people, relationships are created. These relationships progress gradually from being acquaintances to friends to something deeper. The people you meet and interact with may be from the same locality or country as yours, of the same thoughts and values as yourself or someone entirely different both culturally and with regard to their belief system. Taking into account all of these varied facets, theorists have classified social capital into different types. There are three main types of social capital, namely, bonding social capital, bridging social capital, and linking social capital. Let's take a look at all of these three types in detail below.

1. BONDING SOCIAL CAPITAL

This refers to a relationship between two people that are similar to one another. The similarity could be anything that helps to create a bond between people. It could be your age, your hobbies, interests, relationship status, your career aspirations, your profession, the industry you work in, or your philosophies about business. When two people have something in common, networking and building a relationship becomes much easier. The point of connection serves as a foundation for the relationship and provides a good start to it. Bonding leads to the formation of a very close relationship between two people and is therefore considered to be the strongest form of social capital. This can happen between two people or two groups of people who are similar to each other.

While bonding starts because of the commonality two people share with one another, this kind of relationship typically grows and strengthens with time. You might have a colleague at your workplace you spend time with every day; there might be a business associate you speak to quite often because he supplies the stationery you require for your office, or there might be a hotel owner you meet regularly because you use the conference room facility at his property to host meetings. There might be a group of people you bump into oftentimes in the elevator of your office building because they, like you, also have their workplace in there or you might have a set of clients you repeatedly work with from time to time. All of these are examples of bonding.

Bonding could also refer to your relationship with your friends, neighbors, or family members. These relationships tend to provide emotional as well as professional support to those who invest in them. Most if not all of the members of such a network are interconnected and know one another. These strong social ties have their foundation in a high level of trust. A deep sense of belonging is often found in these dense networks of people. One important characteristic of bonding social capital is that the relationships formed in this method involve repeated interaction among people. You will need to meet the person over and over again for an extended period of time in order for a bond to be created. As a consequence, these relationships most often only develop between people from the same community or group.

This is because it is the people of our community that we meet the most on a daily basis. Bonding can therefore be described as a horizontal inward looking closed network of people. The well-known sociologist Robert Putman in his book *Bowling Alone* says, "Bonding is good for getting by in life." In most circumstances, the people you have a strong deep bond with are also those who belong to the same social class as your own. As a result of this, a network of bonded individuals gel very well with one another, share knowledge, and extend support and help when needed. When we have a bond with someone, we do everything in our power to help them and even go out of our way to get something done for them; and this behavior is at the heart of a bonding relationship.

2. BRIDGING SOCIAL CAPITAL

What comes to mind when you think of a bridge? It is a passage that connects two places, i.e., two buildings or two pieces of land that are otherwise unconnected. Bridging social capital does something very similar. It is the creation of relationships between two groups of people that are not directly linked with each other. The linking of a neighborhood association with the police department in the area is bridging in action. Unlike bonding, which takes place between groups, bridging happens across groups. In the words of Robert Putman, bridging is a network that can help you get ahead in life. Relationships are formed with the help of an intermediary. For example, your colleague introduces you to a friend of his and a relationship builds between the two of you. This colleague acts as a bridge between the two of you, thereby serving as the cause for the creation of bridging capital. It brings together two parties that would otherwise not connect. These connections typically come from friends of friends, friends of colleagues and associates, relatives of a neighbor, colleagues of a friend who is a business owner, or a client of a family member.

The ties between people in such networks are not as strong as they are in bonding relationships. Since two people are introduced to one another through an intermediary, the links are relatively weak here. One important feature of a bridging relationship is diversity. Simply put, it is a set of horizontal ties between unlike groups. Connections here are formed between more diverse groups of people when compared to bonding. For instance, politicians hang out with other politicians who introduce them to more politicians. While these people might be similar to one another in certain ways, they are not as similar as the kind of people you would find in a bonding relationship. This form of social capital bridges the gap between people of different religions, races, and other factors that divide society. These people usually have shared interests or goals, but differ with regard to their social identities. Despite the differences between them, they are quite similar to one another in terms of their power and social status. While friendships are usually considered bonding relationships, relationships between people of different age groups or cultural backgrounds are categorized as bridging relationships. Since the connection between people in this form of relationship isn't so close and strong, the level of trust between them is also not as deep as you would find in a bonding contact. The weak ties in a bridging relationship however are considered to be the strength of this form of social capital as they allow flexibility in relationships. These relationships are not bound by social sanctions, allowing people the freedom to maintain them for as long as they like and to get rid of them whenever they wish to. People living in urban areas tend to have stronger bridging capital when compared to bonding capital, and it is the opposite for rural communities. Bridging capital is rarely a source of emotional support but because of the diversity in the relationships, it could be of great help to a business owner or anyone else investing in it.

3. LINKING SOCIAL CAPITAL

This is the third and final type of social capital and is different from the two aforementioned ones. The main characteristic feature of this relationship is its vertical nature. So what does this imply? Linking capital includes relationships between people or groups of people who are different from one another in social position or power. Building linking capital would entail forming relationships with people who are more powerful than you. This power could be a result of wealth, position in society, or professional or career standing. Power differences between people are a conscious part of this network. A patron and client relationship or mentor and mentee relationship are some examples of linking capital. These people in power can come from any industry or sector, religious or community groups, business organizations, legal institutions, schools, public agencies, and political groups.

Building a relationship with people in authority can provide access to power and a wide variety of resources that would otherwise not be available to you. Respect and trust are two of the key characteristics of such relationships. These powerful people also expect reciprocity, i.e., mentors would expect their advice and teachings to be used in a good way and to be passed on to others, high net worth individuals providing the funding would want their contribution to make a difference, and so on. Relationships such as these are built to get access to resources, jobs, services, or opportunities. Linking social capital takes a very long time to develop. Creating long-term trusting ties with people in power requires time and frequently even the involvement of intermediaries to catalyze the process. Linking is, in a sense, an extension of bridging social capital. As opposed to the horizontal nature of networks you would find in a bridging relationship, linking involves the formation of vertical bridges between people and groups. While bridging typically occurs between people of a similar socio-economic group, linking takes place between two or more socio-economic groups. A socio-economic group is simply a community and linking takes place between such communities. For example, soccer players often move around and interact with other soccer players and sportsmen. When a soccer player is introduced to a farmer, that's linking in action. Both of these people come from entirely different backgrounds, goals, and interests but can benefit from one another in a myriad of different ways. This relationship could provide the farmer as well as the soccer player with resources and knowledge they wouldn't otherwise receive. Linking can also help bring together people from different classes. For example, the people of the upper class and the lower class rarely mingle and socialize with one another but linking capital can provide both with this opportunity. The relationship between the CEO of a company and a lower-level employee is another example of linking capital. This vertical bridge between these two people can be beneficial to both. The CEO will be able to learn what it is like to work at the bottom level of the company and the employee can receive a lot of valuable advice and acquire knowledge from his superior.

All of these three types of capital are social assets for an entrepreneur. Social capital can help explain why certain firms experience superior managerial performance or efficient supply chains when compared to others, why some businesses are better suited for mergers and acquisitions instead of others, and so on. Social capital is present everywhere in our daily lives, and it is up to us to take advantage of it. Some business owners, however, close themselves to this idea or create a lifestyle for themselves that doesn't allow for the development of social capital. The first and foremost problem is the reluctance to share information. Sharing ideas, knowledge, and resources for the benefit of one another is a key part of networking. In fact, this is one of the prime reasons why people wish to build social capital. This unwillingness to communicate freely with one another is called the "silo mentality", and is often seen among business owners. When the entrepreneurs leading the organization themselves begin to behave in this way, the door of social capital is closed for them forever. Silos can negatively affect workflows and can also impact the overall performance of the enterprise. No business is an island. Successful entrepreneurs always encourage a free flow of information between organizations and are also open to the idea of sharing knowledge and resources with other entrepreneurs and corporate professionals. Communicating is the only way in which solutions to problems can be brought about, and this can never be achieved in an iron curtain organization in which entrepreneurs have a silo mentality. So why do some entrepreneurs behave in this way and what can a business owner do to correct this?

The word silo refers to storage containers used for the purpose of accumulating grains or missiles. In this context, it metaphorically symbolizes those entities that stockpile information and restrict sharing. These entities are typically an entire organization as a whole and tend to operate in complete isolation. If every business in the world and every entrepreneur out there begins to adopt this line of thinking and starts keeping all their knowledge to themselves, building social capital would become a nearly impossible task.

Two major reasons are at the root of this mentality. The first one is competition between business owners. The human ego doesn't permit the other man to be more successful, and not sharing helpful information or trade secrets with anyone serves as a way to satisfy this ego and prevent any plausible achievement or good performance by people on the other end. This can most commonly be seen between businesses of the same industry and businesses directly or indirectly competing with one another. Aside from the ego clash, the silo mentality reflects a narrow vision that such people possess. Hoarding information for their personal benefit and prioritizing self-interest over company goals and objectives, wanting to perform every activity themselves without sharing information with employees are some characteristics of behavior that stem from a silo mentality.

The second reason behind such a mentality is the system of the business itself. Some businesses structure their departments in a way that information cannot freely flow in and out of these organizations due to system limitations. In the rush of creating systematic functions to operate their business, they end up restricting communication and preventing creativity and innovation within their organization and profitable partnerships between business entities. This kind of limiting behavior originates at the top of the organization. Whatever the reason behind the silo mentality, it exists because entrepreneurs allow it to. Those working in such an organization fail to realize the value the information they're sitting on could create for others. They are so blurred by their narrow vision that they aren't able to look at the bigger picture. Every entrepreneur has a critical role to play in the accomplishment of the wider mission of the organization as well as the community at large, but they tend to disregard this. The lack of inter-business and cross-industry communication then affects operational efficiency and profitability because many businesses end up working with inaccurate and outdated information.

Silo mentality is the greatest sin for any organization and for the growth of social capital. Even the best networking strategy, initiative, or plan will not bear fruit if there is a lack of proper communication among people. The business owner needs to be able to let go of the urge of trying to do everything themselves and share their vision with the employees of the organization to help fulfill it. A business owner and their employees can never be self-sufficient. There will always be the need to involve people from the outside to efficiently fulfill the activities of a business. Encouraging proper communication within an organization will ensure its efficient management by its employees, and this will mean more time for an entrepreneur to build social capital. Business owners often make the mistake of working in their business rather than on it and this gives rise to a whole lot of problems both for the entrepreneur as well as their organization. You, as a business owner, should ask yourself this question, "Can I take a 7-day vacation without my mobile phone or any other communication device?", "Can my business operate without me?" If you answered "no" to both of the above questions, then your organization and you are not equipped and ready to build your social capital. You are self-employed and not an entrepreneur yet.

When you are self-employed, you end up spending a lot of your time on the day-to-day activities of your business, leaving very little for you to invest in areas like marketing, streamlining processes, and most of all, building your network. During the early days of a business, when everything is new and nascent, it is understandable for a business owner to be engulfed in routine operations. This, however, should change as the business moves from being a fledgling one to a slightly mature organization. Working on their business, as opposed to working in it, will help business owners spot opportunities and will also enable them to identify areas in which improvement is required. Once their venture becomes self-reliant, they will have ample time to grow their enterprise and their social capital as well. Business owners should aim at and work towards getting to this level instead of becoming caught up in the hampster wheel of day-to-day operations.

Preparing oneself to build social capital is as important as undertaking the activities required to do so. Oftentimes, entrepreneurs jump into networking with a closed mind. They seek knowledge, resources, and opportunities, but do not wish to share any of these with others. Some do not have the time to socialize and attend networking events due to the way their organization is managed, and many just take the plunge into networking without really making any efforts to improve communication and the attitude towards sharing within their enterprise. Entrepreneurs must take the time to assess if they are ready to take on the activity of networking before putting their feet into it. Building social capital isn't easy. It demands the investment of time and effort. Social capital, if accumulated and managed well, could be your trump card to entrepreneurial success and profitability. A wallet full of powerful business cards can sometimes turn out to be your priciest possession, but the same could end up becoming an unwanted pile of trash if the required efforts aren't taken to manage this asset. As Luke Granger rightly said, "A task half done is equal to none." So, "Engage your brain before you engage your weapon," as James Mattis said.

After introducing you to the concept of social capital and providing you with an understanding of how important it is to be prepared before working on building it for yourself, it is now time to uncover all of the different ways in which you can benefit from it. So, read on and get ready to be amazed!

CHAPTER TWO:
. . . .

BENEFITS OF SOCIAL CAPITAL

Having come this far in this book, you have a good understanding of what social capital actually is and why it is important to invest in it. You might, however, be wondering how this so-called goldmine can benefit an entrepreneur like you as you go about managing and growing your business. Every business owner is likely to face scenarios along their journey in which there will be questions that need to be answered in order to progress. As a natural response to such a circumstance, most entrepreneurs will put in everything they individually have to find a solution. But it is humanly impossible for anyone in this world to have answers to everything. What does one do when faced with a situation like this one? Contact someone you know who could be resourceful on the subject and ask for help. Your chances of finding a successful way out will be closely related to the number and quality of people you know. The process of finding a solution might sometimes be easy and at other times more difficult, but a solution will surely come out of this exercise in most cases.

Social capital or networking really is the end all of your journey to becoming a great entrepreneur. There are so many things you cannot do on your own that even thinking about them can be overwhelming. The good news, however, is that you don't have to. Social capital will open doors to opportunities you did not know you can access. So, what are they? Here are some ways in which social capital can benefit a business owner like you.

1. IT CAN HELP RAISE FUNDS

Businesses have a large number of financial needs. Every stage in the growth cycle brings new needs. When you are stuck in a scenario in which you are in urgent need of funds and all that you have is locked up in your business already, a bunch of useful connections can help put together the required sum of money in no time. Two or three of your entrepreneur friends might agree to jointly provide you with a personal loan, or alternatively, a friend of someone you know might help you get in touch with an angel investor. Just some basic advice from one of your contacts might help you find a way to probably bring down the cost or find a cheaper alternative to what you need for your business. The possibilities are endless. As varied as entrepreneurs and their ventures are, as are their ideas, experiences, and thought processes. You never know which opinion might turn out to be a game changer for you in your business. As you meet new people and discuss your business concept with them, you might bump into someone voluntarily wishing to associate with you by way of a financial contribution out of mere interest in your idea.

Raising funds is most often a tricky business for entrepreneurs the world over. To be able to convince someone to invest a buck in your idea at a stage in your business when none of the sections of your balance sheet are impressive or when you don't even have one can be quite a task. Your contacts could be a really useful starting point in such a scenario. Even if you plan to go the traditional way to bring in funding for your venture by applying for a bank loan, your likelihood of getting approval will improve if you have a connection with someone at the bank of your choosing. It is true that the key to securing alone ultimately lies in the strength of your idea, but a good relationship with someone at the bank can help you in aspects such as how to speed up the loan approval process and tips on drafting a winning loan application. They could also provide you with valuable advice on what you should avoid to maximize your chances of securing a loan, easier ways to get one for your venture, and alternative funding methods for you to consider.

2. AN OPPORTUNITY TO LEARN FROM OTHERS' MISTAKES

When we meet and make connections with other people, there is a lot we get to learn from them. The journey of entrepreneurship is full of risks, twists, and turns. While it is true that every business has its own story and that the future cannot be predicted, knowing about the problems other entrepreneurs like you face can be of great help. Whether it is somebody working in the same industry as you or a totally unrelated one, their experiences can be a sort of guidebook for you.

Let's consider for example that you have just started a business, selling cakes from home. If you have connections with other bakers in your city who have done this before you, their experience can help you more than other research can. There might be a technique to package your cake you don't know about that can help prevent damage during transportation; there might be a set of flavors that people in that city hate, and knowing this could help you avoid waste and costs. There might be stores out there you aren't aware of that sell ingredients at a cheaper price and much more.

Every industry has its own way of doing things, and only those working in it will have the most up-to-date knowledge about it. This is just a simple example, but knowing other entrepreneurs in your industry can save you a lot of time and resources. If you use your connections in the right way, you will not have to waste your time reinventing the wheel. Why make the same mistake that someone else has made before you when there is a way to avoid it? Building rich social capital for yourself could be that way for you. Try to build connections with as diverse a group of people as possible. It's okay if everyone in your circle of contacts isn't from the same industry or career as yourself. Every individual and the job they do have their own value. You may not always be able to realize this value for yourself and your business when trying to establish a relationship at the start. But as Steve Jobs rightly said, "You can only connect the dots looking backward, you will not be able to connect them looking forward." Everything you do and every relationship you get into is sure to culminate into a beautiful story in your life. Knowledge is power, and the same about other people's good and bad experiences in their respective journeys in business could be a savior for you as you go about establishing, running, and growing your enterprise.

Don't overlook the importance of this opportunity. The best way to move forward is to carefully examine what others do well, but also what they don't do well. Not only will you benefit from understanding their successes, but you will also learn how to avoid their costlier mistakes. With that, you'll be able to enjoy smooth sailing in your own venture.

3. IT CAN HELP YOU SET YOURSELF APART

If your customer chooses you over your competitors, this simply means success for your business. So, what is it that a business owner can do to achieve a competitive advantage in the market? The simple answer is, to offer a product or service that consumers want but aren't receiving yet from what's already available out there. While market research can help to uncover information about your industry and assist in the creation of a competitor strategy, nothing compares to the firsthand information you will receive by directly talking to people. The information you obtain from entrepreneurs themselves will most likely be accurate, and you hold a good chance to know about key events and happenings before the outside world finds out. You can then process and use this information to tweak your offering, add or eliminate features, bring out something new, or take the necessary action to help your business stand out.

As your business moves ahead along the growth curve, more and more competitive scenarios will come into play, and you will have to work much harder on staying at the top. Trying to build a connection with someone just at a time when you need their help is most often of no value. Social capital is like an investment. Just like you put your money in real estate, stocks, or any other financial asset with the aim of reaping gains in the future, so should you do with regard to your network. It is always a good idea for an entrepreneur to start working on building their social capital right at the time when they start working on establishing their enterprise. Your position in the market, relative to your competitors, is greatly strengthened when you have a wealth of social capital to support it. Let's try to understand this with the help of an example. You are an entrepreneur who is about to launch a line of shoes targeted at customers suffering from pain in the legs, feet, knees, etc. There are other brands in the market that deal in orthopedic footwear. You are someone who has a long-standing relationship with an orthopedic specialist in the city and decide to involve him in your marketing campaign. Can you imagine how great a competitive advantage one review from an orthopedic doctor about your footwear can provide you? Brands are all about trust and loyalty, and one simple contact can give you both of these for your business. How you translate this consumer interest into permanent loyal customers for your business and whether or not your product is strong enough to sail you through is a subject for another time. But a social connection like this one is sure to garner eyeballs for your brand at the time of launch. The best part, knowing and having a good relationship with an ortho isn't a very difficult task. Success lies in being able to know the right person at the right time and having the sensibility and intelligence to use the right contact in the right way.

4. IT IS AN EASY TOOL FOR MARKETING

As the owner of your business, you are the face of your enterprise. Everything about your business will be associated with you. Whether you are a sole trader, one of the partners in a partnership firm, or the owner of a corporation, you are sure to be considered synonymous with the organization and even more so during its early days. So what does this imply? You are in essence a marketing tool for your venture. When you meet someone in a professional setting, you are directly or indirectly promoting your venture. If you meet one person, that person gets to know about who you are and what you do and if you have a network of 100 people, all of these 100 people do. The greater the size of your contact list, the more people you have to popularize your offering among. Although one-to-one marketing cannot be done at a very large scale and at a very fast pace, it is known to be extremely effective.

While someone would spend a few seconds watching your ad campaign, the level of engagement is much higher when a personal face-to-face interaction is involved. Say, for instance, that you attend a wine and cheese party specifically organized for entrepreneurs. You are most likely to meet a large number of entrepreneurs, but the amount of time you spend with each of them will be much more than a few seconds. One conversation leads to another, and when you happen to develop a bond with somebody there, they will get to know much more than just your name and company information. If all goes right, you might end up sharing details about how you started up and went about establishing your business. A conversation like this will lead to the creation of a story about you in the mind of the listener, and stories are said to be the easiest and most effective way to remember something. They will remember your story and you theirs, and this chain will go on and on with every new networking event you attend. Every instance of publicity, be it small or large, specific or general, will only do good for your business in the long run and your social capital will do this publicity for you. The icing on the cake here is that marketing your business in this way will cost you much less when compared to the thousands and thousands of bucks you will spend on television or newspaper ads. What more would any entrepreneur want than an easy, effective and cheap method of promoting their business? Everything you say about your business and yourself will make an impression in the minds of the people you meet, so it is important that you prepare yourself about how you would like to present your venture beforehand. Like you would work on all the aspects of a television ad right from design to content before it goes on air, you should do the same with yourself as well. Think about what you will say and how you will say it; how the other person might respond, and how you will react to their comments before attending every event. As you go about slowly building your social capital and gradually marketing your business, you will be creating a strong foundation for the future of your enterprise.

5. IT'S A SOURCE OF IDEAS

Business is all about finding answers to the how-tos. No matter how experienced you are in the field you plan to operate your business, the process of running your venture is sure to be a learning curve for you. Every entrepreneur wants to know the best, easiest, and most efficient way to manage their enterprise, and social capital could be the answer for them. So what are those ways in which your connections can be of help to you in this respect? The first is about technology and automation. In the tech-savvy world we live in, a lot of the jobs are now automated. What kind of technology or software should you use for your enterprise based on your industry type? Will option A work better or option B? In the early days of your enterprise, when you are struggling for funds, you do not always have the option to try expensive technology products and trash them if they don't work. Speaking to your fellow entrepreneurs or other people in the industry you have a relationship with can be of great help in this regard. These connections can provide you with ideas about a particular technology or software you aren't aware of. As you go about socializing with them, you might also learn about a new way of using a certain technology product in your office to maximize efficiency, productivity, and profitability. Technology is the tool most entrepreneurs today used to better organize and speed up processes, and social capital can teach you how to make the best use of technology and stay ahead.

Aside from technology, there is a lot more you will have to figure out based on the nature of your business. There might be a certain courier company you don't know of that is better than others to help you with quick deliveries. There might be an organization all the players of your industry are associated with that provides help to entrepreneurs in areas like complying with legal regulations, managing the business, or managing employees.

As you meet people, interact with them, and learn about how they are managing their business, you will surely be able to come up with ideas for improving your management style. If you have connections with people in other industries, communities, or countries, there might be something interesting there in that other world with regards to marketing, business development, product development, or anything else which you could apply in your own business and industry. Meeting new people always gives rise to new thought processes, newer ways of looking at things, and eventually new ideas. These thinking patterns can lead to innovation in your business in terms of the way you solve your problems, the kind of products and services you produce, the way you sell your offering, and the way you formulate strategies.

6. IT'S A SUPPORT SYSTEM DURING TURBULENT TIMES

Whether you are an aspiring entrepreneur or an experienced one, you surely know that running a business is never a smooth ride. No matter how much you plan, establishing and managing your enterprise is not going to be a bed of roses. This might sound a bit pessimistic, but it is unfortunately the reality every successful business professional in the world will agree with. As you move along the path of entrepreneurship, there will be times when things won't go your way. You might falter and fall. The road to success hasn't been easy for any notable accomplished person in history. During these trying times, what you will need the most is support. So how can your connections help you in such circumstances?

First and foremost, they can provide you with valuable advice. A person who is more knowledgeable and experienced than you will be able to tell you just what to do when faced with a tricky scenario. Such words of wisdom can prove invaluable to any entrepreneur feeling like fish out of water in any circumstance. What's more, a bonding relationship with a person or set of people can be a great source of emotional support when life seems unfair or you happen to face a setback in your career. Relationships like these can help to pick you up after a failure. Entrepreneurs are generally strong, resilient personalities that do not give up easily, but a rainy day is an inevitable part of life, and social capital is that resource that can bring back the sunshine to your world.

Staying motivated is another prerequisite for success in the business arena. The rate at which businesses fail is high, no matter which part of the world you live in. To be able to cross every stumbling block and persevere until you reach a point of stability and profitability in your venture requires immense determination and passion. Your social capital could be a perennial source of both of these and much more for you. Seeing others around you sail through the difficult times and come out victorious will give you the strength and confidence to do the same with your business. Receiving positive feedback or appreciation from someone experienced or knowledgeable during a difficult phase in your business can be extremely encouraging, and the connections you build can do that for you. Every new person you meet and every new story you listen to could be a great source of inspiration for you in your entrepreneurial journey. It is said that every person is an average of the people they spend the most time with. So, surrounding yourself with a network of positive, upbeat, passionate, ambitious, and strong people will surely fill your life with optimism and light, thereby helping you in a myriad of different ways as you go about growing your enterprise.

Building a business is not a one-day activity. It is therefore essential that you have a good support system with you throughout in order to keep you going. All the people in your network will not be of the same kind. While some will be able to provide you with advice and guidance, others might be a source of emotional strength. All in all, a combination of all kinds of connections is what you need as an anchor for your business when the weather gets stormy.

7. IT INCREASES YOUR HAPPINESS QUOTIENT & PROMOTES GOOD HEALTH

Entrepreneurs work very hard to establish their businesses. Long days, sleepless nights, missing meals, back-to-back meetings, frequently hopping between different cities and sometimes even countries - these are normal occurrences in the life of a business person. While all, if it is required to fulfill your entrepreneurial dream, not taking care of your physical and mental health can ruin everything in a flash. All humans are social beings. They crave connection, love, and bonding. In the rush of setting up their business, entrepreneurs often forget or begin to ignore this need of theirs. What ultimately results from this is unhappiness, dissatisfaction, and illness. What is the point of working hard on your business when the end result isn't bringing you happiness? Many entrepreneurs around the world make the mistake of working day in and day out despite not feeling good about it. This kind of lifestyle is not only detrimental to your physical and mental health but will also not allow you to go on with what you're doing for long. Your body will stop supporting you in the activities you would be required to undertake in order to realize your dream, and you will be left with no option but to stop.

It is believed that networking is directly linked with improved health and increased levels of happiness. Positive social relationships are known to promote a positive mindset and improve satisfaction with life. Entrepreneurs are inherent dreamers and achievers, but a happy and healthy entrepreneur is more likely to be able to accomplish their targets when compared to someone who is ill or unhappy in life. Work on building your social capital, and you will feel joy and positive feelings flowing into your life, and this will, in turn, result in the creation of an entrepreneurial success story for you.

Good health is crucial for everyone but even more so for entrepreneurs. When you dedicate yourself to growing your business, you expand a lot of energy in the process. As such, you need to always keep your health at the forefront of your mind. Good nutrition is essential. Do not skip meals, or worse, reach for the easy options of junk food and energy drinks. Moreover, exercise regularly. By exercising, we're not suggesting that you hit the gym seven days a week (although that's great if you do), but you should aim for light exercise, like going for a walk, daily.

When you network, you'll find yourself with more time to take care of yourself as suggested above, so it's the best way to take care of your health.

8. IT CAN OPEN THE DOOR TO OPPORTUNITIES

If you want to be a successful entrepreneur, just work on knowing as many people as possible. This might seem surreal to some and too simplistic to be able to yield useful results to other people, but it is true. Opportunities only come from people. Every entrepreneur needs people to get their job done. Just assume for a moment that you have a great business idea in your mind. You are extremely excited about it and spend a lot of time researching it. What you have in mind is a product, a sort of technological innovation. There is none like it in the market, and it has the potential to fill a huge need. You, however, realize that you do not have the technical expertise to make this idea tangible. The world of software and machines is alien to you, but you are not the kind to give up. What would you do? The first thing most people would attempt in a circumstance like this one is to think if they know someone who can help them with their task, and if you happen to come up with a name from your contacts who possess the expertise to help you, here is an opportunity you have created for them. So what does this example indicate? All it takes to get an opportunity is to know a person who needs something to be done.

There is no magic and there are no fairies, so it is impossible for us to read someone's mind. However, we can try to build strong connections with as many people as possible so that we end up in the right mind at the right time at least sometimes. So what kind of opportunities can you expect to receive from your network? As the owners of a profit-making enterprise, entrepreneurs always expect a monetary gain from everything they undertake.

This isn't by any chance an unreasonable expectation, but you should remember that profit can come looking in different ways. It isn't always necessary that you will find someone wanting to hire your service or purchase your product from among the people you know. Certain activities, such as accepting an invitation to speak at a college convocation or sponsoring an event for a person you know, might not give you any direct benefit, but can bring you other unexpected gains. For example, one of the students at a college might end up working for you as a sales manager contributing hugely to your bottom line, a man you sponsored might introduce you to someone influential who might in turn go on to bring in profitable deals for your business, you might find a suitable business partner to work with, someone might offer to buy you out at a good price, you might get the opportunity to get into a merger with a magnanimous megacorp, or the people you are interacting with for no direct monetary gain right now might refer your products/services to others thereby bringing in sales for you. Think about all those times in life when an opportunity came your way. If you look at that situation closely, you will notice that directly or indirectly there would have been the involvement of someone you know. The harder you work on building and maintaining your social capital, the greater will be your chances of receiving opportunities from them. Success in business is a combination of selflessness and foresight. If you use your social capital keeping in mind both of these attributes, selflessly helping the people of your network in whichever way you can, and being able to plan your actions in accordance with some amount of forethought about what the future might hold, your network can do wonders for you.

9. IT CAN ELEVATE YOUR IMAGE

We all know someone around us who is like a hero for getting things done. Have a problem? That person will be able to help. Need something? They can arrange it for you. People like these are able to accomplish all of this only with the help of the connections they have in every sphere of life and nearly every stratum of society. Such entrepreneurs are looked upon very highly by those around them and often tend to enjoy a superior public image. They are portrayed as leaders in their circle. This positive image helps them to win the trust of other business professionals and entrepreneurs around them, and where there is trust, there is greater scope for collaboration. If given a choice, anyone would like to only associate with those people they trust. When a lot of people and businesses begin to trust an entrepreneur, it leads to the creation of goodwill and a positive reputation for who they are and what they do.

The benefits that come with intangible assets such as these are plenty and are hard to quantify. If you manage to achieve such high levels of popularity and trust, you will most likely be able to garner a greater volume of business, receive a longer credit repayment period from your suppliers, have easy access to the best in the industry to meet your business needs, and have things your way in many if not all of the activities you undertake.

So, these were some of the major benefits one can expect to receive from their social capital. Isn't it remarkable how much people and relationships can contribute to the growth, profitability, and success of an enterprise? Your network is in many ways your true net worth. This intangible resource that is built up through social interactions helps people to work together in a group to fulfill a common purpose and facilitates the formation of networks of trust and cohesion in society. Social capital theory suggests that social relationships once formed can benefit individuals and organizations beyond their original context of creation.

Social capital is a metaphor for other types of capital. It is an invest-ment in trustworthy networks and social relations that enables collabora-tion and provides a multitude of other benefits. The value of social capital lies in its ability to transfer and facilitate other forms of capital beneficial for entrepreneurs and their businesses. The advantages of social capital shine through only after it is mobilized, and as a system, it feeds on itself. Trusting relationships help build other trusting relationships, and the chain goes on.

After all that we have discussed so far, one point presents itself boldly and clearly. Social capital is the most important of the three capital types. As a business owner, the larger your sphere of influence, the easier will be your road to success. This resource has the power to simplify and improve every-thing you attempt. If you have a large network and you are in need of capital to expand, your network would bring potential investors or connections to them in a way better than a random search for the same in unknown terri-tory would. If you have an urgent need to hire someone for a specific open position in your enterprise and you present this need to your network, they will most likely refer you to a better business professional than someone responding to the position through an ad or online forum.

Let me share with you one of the many instances in which my social capital has helped me. In my job as an entrepreneur and business coach, I once had a client who was a real estate investor. He was highly successful at flipping homes. One day, he called me very concerned. He had purchased two homes at an auction at a great price, but he had a major problem. He was highly undercapitalized due to the two purchases. Since I had built up my social capital over the years, I decided to test it. I approached my contacts and told them all that my client is in dire need of $100,000 to flip two of his homes. Within a matter of two hours, I had two investors ready and willing to invest the $100,000. A job that would otherwise take days or even weeks was completed just in a space of a few hours, and my client was very happy with the deal. The wealth of connections I had amassed not only helped me to solve my client's problem but also strengthened my relationship with him, thereby bringing me more business opportunities and a better reputation in the market. One activity involving just a few phone calls gave me that asset which only years of hard work and toil can. This is the unbelievable power of this amazing resource we call social capital.

We have talked enough about the benefits of building your social capital. It is now time to tell you how you can create a resource like this for yourself and change your life for the better.

CHAPTER THREE:
· ·

HOW TO BUILD SOCIAL CAPITAL

All this while, we have been discussing what social capital is and how useful it can be for your career, but take a moment to think about this. What do you precisely want your network to do for you? All the benefits you read about in the previous chapter are the end result and we all want those for our business, but what would it take on the part of your contacts to make that happen? The first and most important thing is that your connections must be willing to speak for you. Social capital is not just about collecting business cards and filling up your phone book. You might know a hundred people, but this will have no meaning if they aren't willing to talk for you when needed. Social capital increases when you connect, give, share, care, value, and trust, and none of these will be of any meaning if communication isn't involved. Let me explain this with the help of an example. You join a networking organization in your local area and build connections with a few people. Your objective behind taking this membership is obviously to grow your profits and expand your business. So, at one of the events, you decide to speak to one of your contacts who you think can help get your product on the shelves of a large retail chain. This retailer has about 500 stores all across the country, and this deal could be a huge boost to your business if it clicks. You are very sure this man has the necessary influence and power to get this done for you, but you will only realize the gain if the man actually decides to speak to the owner of the retail store for you. So what does this illustrate? The willingness to help is a very vital ingredient if you aspire to extract any kind of benefit from your social contacts.

It's important to understand that you also need to find your own way of building social capital. What works for one person may not work for the next. Because of this, what we're suggesting below are broad ways of building your social capital. You'll probably find that a combination of all these methods will work best for you.

Knowing that social capital can help a business thrive is one thing, but actually making those relationships happen is another ball game. Below are a few steps you can take to build your social capital in a way that proves beneficial to you and your business.

1. MAKE YOURSELF WORTHY

When you as an entrepreneur decide to step out in the hunt for productive relationships to grow their social capital, they would obviously want to only build ties with people who could be beneficial to them in some way or the other. Likewise, other entrepreneurs and business professionals would want to associate with you only if they feel that you will be able to add real value to their businesses and life. Before you take up the task of building your social capital, take a moment to ponder. What is it that you can offer to the people who you network with? Do you have something using which you can make the lives of other entrepreneurs better in some way? There are a number of things you could possess that can make you worthy of connection. You might have a specialized skill, your experience could turn out to be valuable, or you might have a mighty bank account. Take a moment to think about what you can offer.

Having a good understanding of what your positives are and how valuable you as a contact could be for somebody will help you to better plan your interactions and present yourself well. Writing down is a good way to organize your thoughts clearly. Pull out a sheet of paper, and list all of your accomplishments to date. You could even include your strengths and positive traits. Try to look from the lens of the opposite person. What out of these would be impressive to them? Think strategically and don't be disappointed if you don't find something straight away. You would be meeting a wide variety of people, and all of these will have a wide variety of needs and aspirations. Pick out the items from the list that seem the most attractive, and create a plan to sharpen or polish those that have the potential to yield you great benefits in your networking journey. While it is important to have some solid attributes or achievements to attract people, presenting yourself in an exciting manner is equally essential. In the digital world we live in, having a strong social media presence is key for every entrepreneur. You must have an impressive profile on LinkedIn and other online forums that are popular among business professionals in your area. Do everything you can to show the world that you are worthy of being a part of their social circle. There are broadly two ways to grow your social capital. The first is to approach people yourself, interact with them and work to build meaningful relationships with them and the second is to make yourself so attractive as a prospective contact that others are forced to take the first step to establish a connection with you. You will most likely have to adopt a combination of these two approaches unless you are a born celebrity, belong to an influential family, or are some gifted prodigy. Its degree of importance might vary a little, but preparing and shaping yourself is a prerequisite in both approaches.

2. TRY TO KNOW AS MANY PEOPLE AS POSSIBLE

A network is a cluster of relationships between different people, and each one of these relationships begins with meeting others. Relationships form and trust flourishes only when you know people. Every person you interact with will not turn into a useful and profitable social connection, but the greater the number of people you know, the higher will be your chances of finding the right kind and quality of relationships. Knowing people is no rocket science; you have been doing it since you were very young. There are so many people you already know irrespective of who you are or what you do in life. You don't need to converse with them for hours every day or try to become best pals, you only need to take a dip into their world, so to speak. What is required of you at this point in time is to work towards knowing new people in a more conscious way. Even if you do nothing, life will automatically cause you to meet new people and build new relationships, but you do not have all the time in the world to create your entrepreneurial success story.

Think about the strongest relationships you have in your life apart from those with your family members. Take a moment to recap how you managed to develop such a bond with this person. Where did you meet them? What was the icebreaker moment? How did your story start? Which qualities or characteristics drew you towards that person? What did you do to take the relationship forward? Most of our relationships happen so organically that we don't actually realize everything that went into their creation. Whatever you do in the course of your life, both at the professional and personal level, you will most often have two choices: to do it with the people you already know or to go out of your comfort zone and explore new possibilities with those who are strangers to you. Try to indulge in the latter as much as possible. Make it your goal to meet new people periodically. Having a target will help a great deal. For example, decide for yourself that you will meet 60 new people in the next month. Set aside a page in your diary to keep a record of the same. Write down the name of the person along with a brief note about their career standing. Seeing this list will not only motivate you but will also increase the feel-good quotient in your system and keep you on track to achieve your larger goal of building your social capital. This might sound like a very basic exercise to perform, but a simple greeting or small talk is always, or at least in most cases, the starting point of a relationship. As you go about living your life and managing your business, keep this at the back of your mind. Try to do every activity of life with a new person each time as much as possible. Whether you are at the gym, at the airport, at a conference, or in the process of finalizing a contractor for your business, attempt to find someone new to interact with and work with.

This task is like sowing a seed. Whether or not it germinates and sprouts into a beautiful plant depends upon various factors including how you care for it, but you can never expect to have a plant without a seed. The concept of relationships is likewise. All of the seeds you sow by knowing more and more people will grow over time to create for you a rich and dense forest of relationships and a wealth of social capital as a result.

3. BE AT THE RIGHT TIME IN THE RIGHT PLACE

Relationships are all about timing. A lot of factors go into making a relationship click; so what does the right time mean? For a business owner, any event that brings together other entrepreneurs like yourself would be the right time and place. You need to be out there, attending, contributing, and participating in events. These events don't necessarily have to be focused on business alone. Interacting with people in an informal setting such as a cafe, club, or sports center and talking to them on subjects other than work helps in the creation of strong bonded relationships. Career-related conversations are important, but light and happy non-work chatting is believed to be a faster way of building a bond with someone.

Look around your community and enquire about the various social organizations present there. Carry out some research about each of their features, what do they offer? What is the joining fee and what would be the other associated costs? How many events do they have in a year? Pick the ones you like the most and join those. It's best to stick to one or two initially. Choose your organizations with care, after systematically evaluating your own needs against what they can offer. Think about your interests and keep the focus on your career standing when selecting organizations. Try to be clear about the kind of organization you wish to join, and you will be surprised at how many options you can find. There are organizations that are gender specific, and joining those could be a great source of support for you especially if you are a woman. Different industries also have their own professional groups and forums. For example, there could be an association of business owners in the telecommunication industry in your area, or there might be an organization focused on women bakers. Spending a good amount of time on research is key here. All of these enrolment procedures are quite easy to complete. The difficult part is the one ahead. Many business owners get it right when it comes to joining networking organizations, but aren't able or willing to attend events regularly.

With the advent of modern methods of communication and socializing, a lot of networking efforts around the world have shifted online. This transition has made the entire relationship-building process very convenient. Entrepreneurs no longer have to restrict themselves to their local communities when trying to build their social capital. All of these advancements are sure beneficial, but face-to-face meetings are believed to be the most effective way to build a relationship. When you start off working on a connection, make it a point to meet them in person a few times during the early days. The first impression is very important when it comes to building a relationship with someone, and online meetings can somewhat distort your real image, thereby squashing the possibility of an ideal start. A lot of nuances, such as body language, are lost when you meet someone online as opposed to in a club lounge or cafe. Once you know the person to a certain degree and you are confident that they too hold a positive image about you in their minds, online conversations via video or text could work as a nice way to maintain the relationship. The possibility of misunderstandings and miscommunication is much higher in online interaction, and you don't want this to crack the foundation of your relationship. So keep the idea of face-to-face meetings alive in your relationships and treat it as the primary mode of communication. If the person you are trying to network with belongs to a different geographical location and an in-person interaction isn't possible, opt for a video call and follow it up with a personal meet-up at the earliest available opportunity.

4. DON'T HESITATE TO TAKE THE INITIATIVE

Maintaining a social connection is about give and take. You do a favor for someone, and the other returns it back to you in a different form and at a different time. This is what networking is all about. It is, however, important that you do not try to calculate your moves. Many people often hesitate to take the first step hoping that the other person must do it. When you are at a networking event, don't wait for someone to come and greet you. The world of socializing is a self-service zone. Nobody is going to make you feel involved if you do not attempt to do it yourself. Take, for instance, that you visit a social event for entrepreneurs. There are a lot of business professionals in attendance there. You don't mingle with them too much and stay on the sidelines with the expectation that your career standing will automatically draw the other attendees towards you. A strategy like this one is sure to misfire because the world isn't short of people to connect with. One less person wouldn't make too much of a difference to those at the event. To avoid losing out on opportunities, put your ego aside and go out and about to speak to people.

5. CONSIDER VOLUNTEERING

Is there a cause that particularly interests you or is close to your heart? Take some time out to associate with organizations that support and work to advance these causes. Whether it is mental health, helping the poor, supporting the elderly, spending time with orphaned children, working towards making the planet a better place, or just encouraging sport or art in your local area, finding people and organizations that work in these areas is easy. When you donate your time to something without expecting any kind of monetary benefit from it, there is a lot you can gain. You will meet a bunch of like-minded individuals that might help enrich your social capital. The activities you do will help build goodwill for you among the people in your area. This goodwill can translate into more valuable relationships and opportunities for your business in the future. If you are not the kind to roll up your sleeves for performing on-site community service, try to contribute in whichever way you find comfortable based on your skills, knowledge, and experience. There are plenty of organizations out there that need knowledge workers to donate their writing, legal expertise, communication skills, and design knowledge. Technology has become an integral part of the operation of every organization around the globe today, and charities and nonprofits are not alien to this way of working. If you fancy yourself as a tech-savvy individual or a master of handling complicated computer programs and sophisticated software, you can volunteer to provide these services to community organizations in and around your locality when you have the time. Extending voluntary mentorship services to students and upcoming entrepreneurs is also a great way to do your part in the improvement of trade and commerce in the world. All of the little efforts you make to serve society will further improve your reputation and help you get ahead in your career. You will be surprised to see the wealth of social capital you are able to accumulate while performing the simple act of spreading smiles. Support is a beautiful thing. By giving it to the people who need it the most in the form of your time, you will not only make strong social connections but will also end up feeling good.

6. BECOME A MENTEE

We as entrepreneurs are never complete and self-sufficient as far as knowledge and experience are concerned. No matter which stage of your career you are in, getting the help of a mentor is never too late. Doing so will not only provide you with a ton of valuable wisdom but can also help you build a good relationship with a great person in your field. As you spend more and more time with this person, you will also have an opportunity to learn how they went about building their social capital. One connection leads to another, and a strong relationship with your mentor can also introduce you to a number of other influential people in the world of business.

When engaging in these activities, always keep an open mind. Being a mentee does not mean that you will take what your mentor says as the rule of the law. Mentors are human beings too, so they also make mistakes, have incorrect opinions, and may sometimes appear misguided. Use your common sense and distance yourself from your mentor's opinions when it becomes clear that you have outgrown them. It is then time to perhaps find a new mentor.

7. PRACTICE RECIPROCITY

Networking revolves around a simple law known as the "law of reciprocity." What does this mean? It's simple. If somebody does you a favor, you must return it with an equal or more amount of generosity if possible. This is the basic rule you should follow if you wish to succeed in your social capital-building effort. Practicing reciprocity isn't difficult at all. Name any popular figure or someone having a deep and rich social network, they all do it. As discussed earlier in the book, intentions are very important when you get into networking. Helping someone with the sole purpose of receiving a favor back from them will not serve you well. Instead of working to your advantage, such an act will have the opposite effect on your social capital. When you act with your own selfish motives, seeing through it isn't hard for anyone. So, if you wish to preserve your goodwill, try to work from a place of integrity. People are nice and they want to help, so be real and keep your efforts consistent.

8. DON'T HESITATE TO ASK FOR HELP

Nobody in the world has ever been able to achieve success at anything all by themselves. Whether it is building a business or your social capital, it's ok to ask for ideas and assistance. Start with your family members and friends, and ask them to introduce you to other people they know. Think strategically about each of your strongest ties, and analyze how much each of them will be able to help you in building your social capital. No matter which profession they are in, have an honest discussion with them about your desire to form new connections and ask them how best they can help. You need not attempt to build relationships with all of their contacts. Speak to them about the people they know, and pick the ones you would want to connect with. Have a notepad and pen with you at all times during such conversations so that you can note down the names of your prospective social connections. Once you have a good enough list, have a personal interaction arranged with each of them. As discussed earlier, always prioritize a face-to-face meeting over an online one. If you feel awkward about meeting these people all alone, you can take the family member or friend who introduced you to them with you on the first rendezvous or two.

There are a few things you will have to think about before you plan the meet-up. The first and foremost aspect is the setting. Do you want this meeting to appear like a planned interaction, or do you want it to come across as an accidental meeting? The option you choose for yourself is a matter of preference, and there is nothing right or wrong about either. Always choose the one in which you will be the most comfortable and at ease. If you would like the meeting to be formal, you will need to inform the opposite party about your interest to interact with them and you will also need to choose the place appropriately. One entrepreneur I know, a pharmaceuticals manufacturer who was just starting out, wasn't comfortable with the idea of a formal planned meeting. The person he was interested in connecting with was his brother Bill's customer-turned-friend. Bill was the owner of a hair salon in the city, and his customer friend was a medical researcher. To tackle the problem, Bill planned a get-together of his friends asking each of them to bring their sibling along for some extra entertainment. This automatically gave Henry an opportunity to meet Bill's friend and form a connection with him. This one meeting translated into enormous opportunities for both of them, and they have now become business associates working together towards the creation of pharmaceutical products for the world at large. Every individual is different, and consequently, their challenges are too. Try to work around them, and make use of the strongest connections in your life to expand your social capital. Every new connection you form can then introduce you to more people leading to the establishment of more connections, and the chain will go on.

9. LOOK INTO THE PAGES OF YOUR PAST

University is the time when we meet a whole lot of new people. Think back to the time when you were a student on campus. There are so many others like you aspiring to make it big in the field you wish to, and you spend three or more years with them. What better start can you ask for to build a relationship? Dig through your phonebook, contact the alumni association of your university, and try to rekindle those relationships. If you were a student pursuing an MBA, you are most likely to find a number of entrepreneurs and CEOs amongst your classmates. The boys and girls you participated with in interdepartmental cultural events might have also attained success in their own respective fields. Finding a diverse mix of contacts is the ultimate aim of anyone wanting to build their social capital, and your university friends and alumni network could help you achieve this quite easily.

You need not restrict your search to the students who studied alongside you in the same batch. Your University Career Centre will be able to provide you with email addresses and mobile numbers of students from other groups and departments as well, like those who attended the same university before and after you. Reaching out to your professors could also be extremely beneficial. They can serve as a guiding hand for you in your entrepreneurial journey whilst also introducing you to a number of other useful contacts. Since you already know your classmates and professors, you will most likely not require any formal introduction. After exchanging some pleasantries, ask them how they can help you in building your social capital. This is most likely not your first interaction with them, so dropping a text or email could also work fine. Even if you have never personally interacted with somebody or have forgotten them, the fact that you come from the same alma mater will serve as an icebreaker. Attend your school and university alumni meetings as often as you can, and you will see your social capital grow in no time. Further to this, if there is any club or group you were associated with in the past, i.e., a travel group with which you toured around a new country or place every year or a summer school you attended, try touching bases with those friends/ acquaintances once again and taking those relationships to the next level.

10. HARNESS THE POWER OF SOCIAL MEDIA

Complete reliance on online tools to build a relationship is definitely not a good idea for those seriously looking to grow their social capital, but using social media to find connections surely is. There are two ways to look for contacts using the internet, and the approach you choose will depend upon whether you specifically know who you are searching for or not. For example, there is an entrepreneur in your city that you recently learned about and would like to connect with him. You've never met him, but you know his name and have a rough idea about his business. In a circumstance like this, you can perform a simple search online and try to look for his email address or mobile number. You can then attempt to schedule a meeting with them using the details you managed to find. Adding this entrepreneur as a friend on Facebook, following them on Instagram, or developing a professional connection with them on LinkedIn could also be a great way to start. Once the online connection has been established, avoid the temptation to immediately start messaging them. While it is true that you are an authentic person, social media is full of hackers and spam. It's quite easy for someone not to take you seriously or believe your word if they don't know you personally. So, your first step should be to somehow prove your genuineness to this entrepreneur. You can do this by sharing information about your business, your website address, links to your LinkedIn profile, or any other detail which you think will serve the purpose. Do not share too much too early, and always remember your boundaries.

In the event that you do not have any particular name in mind, your approach will have to be a little different. You will have to start by looking for Facebook groups for entrepreneurs. You will easily be able to find such local groups in most large cities of the world. Try joining them, and you will have the chance to connect with a large number of like-minded individuals in one place. Joining national or international groups focused on your topic area could also be a great way to expand your reach beyond boundaries. No matter which industry you work in, you will most likely be able to find something for you on Facebook that will help you grow your network. The people you will find in groups like these will be quite similar to you, looking to build their social capital. So, you do not need to feel awkward about communicating with them. Conversations on such platforms are usually to the point, and you have a good chance of making useful relationships and finding opportunities there. It is, however, important that you stay cautious all the way through and use your judgment before entering into any sort of contract with anyone.

Another popular technique that you can use on LinkedIn is to connect with the leaders in your industry and try to form a relationship with them by commenting on their posts. As you continue to interact with them this way, you will be able to create an impression about yourself in their minds. You can then ask them for a meet-up over coffee, and you will be surprised to know that most people say yes.

Staying focused and having a plan are key when it comes to growing your social capital. There are a number of tools available out there that you can use to streamline your efforts. One popular method is to take up a challenge. Set goals for yourself with regard to networking, and prepare action plans to achieve those goals. Before you begin, however, you must answer a few questions.

- What is your short-term career goal?

- What do you aim to achieve with your business in the next three years?

- What are your goals for the next five to ten years? Where do you see yourself at the end of this period?

- On the basis of your ambitions and aspirations for your business, what kind of people do you want to have in your network?

- Where do you think you stand along the scale as far as social capital is concerned? Low, medium, or high?

- Take a look at your network and analyze it. Which areas do you think you are deficient in?

- Do you wish to make connections just within your city, within your country, or at an international level?

- What is working in your network and what isn't?

Try to answer all of these questions with as much honesty and detail as you can. You can take the help of a friend to be with you in the process if you like to have someone along to help organize your thoughts. Once you have answered these questions, you will have a clear idea about where you are and where you want to go with regard to your networking. Building your social capital is about making connections with people you are acquainted with, as well as those you know nothing about. If you are just starting out, focusing your efforts on strengthening the ties you already have could be a good idea. Many entrepreneurs out there use the circle technique to help them organize their networking.

Here's how you can use it for yourself. Take a sheet of paper and draw a circle in the middle. "I am here," this is what you write inside it. Around this central circle, draw three large circles. In the innermost circle, list the names of friends and family members with whom you have the strongest ties. In the second circle, list the names of those people with whom your ties are weaker. You can include anyone, from family members to friends to friends of friends and neighbors here. The last circle will include the names of people with whom you have the weakest ties. Take the time to think and write down as many names as you can in every circle. Once you have the names, half your job is already done. Your goal in this activity is to write down the names of people irrespective of whether or not you have met them in the past. The focus here is to try and strengthen your relationships with those people you can identify with at this stage.

The next step would be to make a networking plan with weekly, fortnightly, monthly and yearly goals. Try to make the plan as detailed as possible. Your plan should include the activity you will undertake to build your relationship with the people you have listed. Start with the second circle and slowly progress to the third one. If you are someone who is comfortable taking on challenges, feel free to start with the outermost circle first. You will only be able to handle/fit in a few people at a time. So, picking a few names from the second and a few from the third could also work well. Once you feel that you have reached a good enough level with all of these people, you can then begin to explore unknown territory. All of these connections can then be used to help you find more connections. As you go about creating your networking plan, be sure to think about your specific commitments. In the rush of achieving a certain goal, we often end up ignoring practical aspects of life, and this eventually throws us off course. Prepare a priority list containing activities that require your time and attention. Remember to fit in both your personal as well as your professional life in this list. When you prepare your priority list, start with the activity that requires your attention the most and work backward from there. Once you are clear about your commitments, add the insights derived from the priority list into your networking plan. A plan created in this way will have a greater chance of seeing the light of success. Remember to formulate a plan that not only looks good but also feels good when implemented.

As you progress in life, your commitments will change and so will your priorities. It is, therefore, essential that you keep reviewing your network plan ever so often. Also remember to go through your priority list, make the necessary changes, and tweak your network plan accordingly. Aside from checking if your network plan aligns with your life circumstances at all times, you will also need to conduct a strategic review of your progress periodically. Carrying out this review once every month would be a good idea. Start by looking at your goals for the previous month and your achievements with regard to them. Below are a few questions you must ask yourself.

- Have I succeeded in what I wanted to achieve this month?

- What strategies did I use to build my network?

- Which of my tactics worked and which ones didn't?

- Were there any mistakes that I must avoid in the future?

- Should I make any changes to my goals for the next month on the basis of how the previous month went?

Use the answers of one strategic review to modify the networking plan for the following period if needed. If you feel a particular way of socializing or communicating hasn't worked quite well for you, this is the time to eliminate that method from your repertoire and replace it with another one that you feel could be more effective. Have someone to help you figure out your standing if you find it difficult to do it yourself.

Building your social capital is not as difficult as it seems. If you use the methods and techniques discussed above on the basis of what matches your individual personality and circumstances, you will definitely be able to find success in your endeavors. Whether you are trying to grow your network in a place you have been living for a long time, somewhere you have just moved in, at a time in your career when you absolutely have no connections, or you're someone who already has a few contacts, the tips and tricks discussed in this chapter are sure to be beneficial to you.

The story of every resource in this world doesn't just end with earning it. When you set up a business or take up a job to make money, you then spend time thinking about where and how to use it. Some people like to splurge on luxuries such as cars and branded products, a few like to save money to buy a home in the future, yet others like to invest in stocks or bonds, and many like to donate money. The approach is different for everyone. One thing that is common amongst everyone, however, is working towards maintaining and managing the resource. When you hire an employee for your business, human resource development and training are always on the horizon. As soon as or even before you have the person on board, you begin planning on how to polish the talent and get the best out of them for the benefit of your business. The same applies to your social capital as well. This resource also needs to be managed and maintained for it to bring you profits and opportunities in your life. Anything in life that you don't pay attention to will wither and wilt, becoming a mere pile of accumulated waste in time, no matter how valuable the resource is.

In the next chapter, we will learn about how you can maintain your social connections in the best possible way to yield the best possible gain out of them. You need to take care of your resources for them to be able to take care of you. Let's learn how to do just that.

CHAPTER FOUR:

....

MAINTAINING YOUR SOCIAL CAPITAL

You have joined a few networking organizations, attended events, met people, and collected a large number of business cards. So, what's next? Is your job of building your social capital done? No. Building a relationship is like growing a plant. What you have done so far using the methods discussed in the previous chapter to identify and meet people is only the start. It's like that part of the plant growing process when you choose the seeds and sow them in the soil. Unless by chance, it is unlikely that the seeds will germinate into a beautiful plant if you do absolutely nothing. Likewise, every relationship too has its own growing cycle and requires being cared for. You cannot expect opportunities to flow into your life just by exchanging a business card with somebody. So, what is it that you need to do? Before we delve into the details, let's first look at the stages every relationship goes through. An awareness of this will put you in a better position to take the right action at the right time as you work towards growing your social capital.

The stages of a relationship are awareness, captivation, and trust (ACT). This acronym indicates that relationships in the social context have three stages. The first stage is awareness. This involves identifying a social connection and introducing yourself to them. Your first interaction with someone would typically fall under this stage. Collecting business cards is a characteristic activity of the awareness stage. In the second stage, you captivate. In this stage, the relationship gets a little deeper when compared to the first stage. As the name suggests, this stage will see people trying to captivate the interest of the other person in order to grow the relationship. This would involve meeting one another and organizing sessions to interact and gel with each other. The third and final stage is trust. When you reach this stage in your relationship, you will see a bond of trust develop between you and your social connection. Where there is trust, there is automatically a willingness to help and a consequent inflow of opportunities for both parties. You can expect your contacts to refer your business to others and get you new customers/clients during this stage.

Take a moment to think about the three stages. All of these would require action from your end for you to be able to progress from one to the other. This action that you will take is the maintenance of your connections in simple terms. Have you faced a situation in life when someone you haven't met in years came up to you asking for help of some kind? What was your feeling at that moment? To what degree were you willing to extend the favor requested? Most people wouldn't respond positively. After all, who would want to do something for someone they barely have any relationship with? This brings us back to the central theme of this chapter. Maintaining a relationship is as important as initiating one. So what exactly does maintenance entail? The example of the plant can be best used to illustrate this. At which stage in a plant's growth cycle do you begin watering it? Just when you need its fruit? No! A plant is watered right from the time the seeds are sown in the ground. Likewise, you must keep communication alive in a relationship even during those times when you have nothing to gain from it. What is important to understand is that a social connection is not just about favors. In fact, you will most likely be unable to exactly predict when and in what way you will require a particular contact in the future. So, whenever you start a relationship with someone, make an effort to prevent it from becoming rusty.

How do relationships become rusty? Well, mostly through a lack of interest. When you work for yourself, there are so many things you need to cover that sometimes things fall by the wayside. This is normal but do not let it affect the hard work you put into growing your social capital. Make sure that you do not let all these relationships you carefully cultivated go stagnant. How do you do that? Here are some things you can do to achieve this.

1. FOLLOW-UP

The first and most important step in the maintenance of a relationship is the follow-up. You met an entrepreneur at a networking event, had a brief conversation, and exchanged business cards. Your next course of action after this should always be a follow-up email or text message. Write them a little note about how nice it was meeting them. If there was something particularly interesting about your talk, add a sentence about that. Finish with a "see you again soon" kind of message.

Keep the text short and crisp. Do not use templates, and always create the message yourself. Be honest, and be you. Whatever your personality type, let it shine through. A letter, no matter how short it is, will always be appreciated by the reader. Keep this follow-up message free from any requests for help. Don't ask for an appointment or any other detail from them at this time. Below is an example of a follow-up message just to give you an idea about how to draft one for your contact.

Dear Mr. Matthews,

It was a pleasure meeting you at the Chamber of Commerce event last Saturday. Your thoughts about the future of lithium in the telecommunications industry and your ambitions for your brand of mobile phone accessories really inspired me. I am looking forward to catching up with you once again at an event and having another great conversation.

Kind regards,
James Walker
Founder and Managing Director
The Walker Shoe Company
(000-000-0000)

Make sure to include your website address and contact number below the email. This kind of simple message will add to and strengthen the impression your contact has about you in their mind.

2. EXCHANGE PLEASANTRIES ON SPECIAL OCCASIONS

How would you feel if you received a bouquet of flowers on your birthday from someone you know? You'd be happy, wouldn't you? Even if you don't speak to that person on a daily basis, a gesture like this would surely bring a smile to your face. Extending your good wishes to your social contacts on their birthday is one effective way of maintaining a relationship with someone. It shows you care, and that you are interested. It however isn't necessary that you choose to send flowers. Just picking up the phone and saying "Happy birthday," or sending a text would also work well. Try to stand out in whatever option you choose. You might have a question at this point, "There are so many people I know, how do I remember each one of their birthdays?" In the digital world we live in, the first thing we do after meeting someone is connect with them on social media. If you are someone who does this with all of your contacts, knowing and remembering birthdays wouldn't be a hassle at all. If, for some reason, you aren't able to find out the birthday of any of your social connections, drop this idea and find other occasions to greet them.

Christmas, New Year, and Thanksgiving are three occasions everyone can take advantage of. Depending on your faith, there might even be more, like Easter or Hannukah. Make it a point to greet your contacts on these festive days in whichever way seems most appropriate to you. There are a number of websites you can use to send greeting cards and gifts on the basis of how much or how little you want to spend. If you aren't the kind to send cards, emails or WhatsApp messages are also good options. Whatever little you do for someone on happy occasions like these does make an impact even if you don't realize it at the time.

3. SHOW INTEREST AND SHOWER PEOPLE WITH COMPLIMENTS WHENEVER POSSIBLE

You open the morning newspaper and find a write-up about the business of one of your acquaintances in the local news section. What would be the right thing to do if you are looking to build your social capital? Anyone who is good at maintaining relationships would send this person a message letting them know that they have read the article. This doesn't literally mean telling them "I read the article about you." Tell them what you liked about it and wish them luck. You could say something along the lines of, "Looks like a really interesting concept. Waiting to learn more! Way to go! Wish you all the luck with your new venture!" You will sometimes have a lot to say and sometimes not a lot, but there will certainly be something that you like and that's what you must mention. You should however be cautious enough to not shower anyone with fake praise. Be real in whatever you say. Everyone likes compliments, but one that isn't genuine isn't hard to spot and could be detrimental to you in your social capital-building effort. If you happen to read a good news story about any of your contacts, congratulate them on it. If you hear something good about someone you know, i.e. they have a good work culture, the CEO is a dynamic leader, or the company is genuinely an equal opportunity organization, make sure to pass on the good word to the person who deserves the credit.

Commenting on and complimenting the posts of your connections on social media is another way to stay on top of someone's mind. Many people express their opinions on these platforms by way of articles and some even have their own blogs on which they share their thoughts and knowledge. Engage with them and add to the conversation by expressing your point of view. This is a great way to create interest and yourself, get noticed by the targeted person and a host of other entrepreneurs and business professionals, and attract people who would want to build a connection with you. When you get involved with such posts on a regular basis, you automatically create conversation starters and opportunities and set the stage for meetings with particular social contacts in the future.

4. SAY, "HELLO!"

The best way to build a strong network is to get in touch with people when you need nothing from them. Nobody likes to be remembered only in a time of need. Pick out two of your contacts daily or weekly depending on how many of them you have, and send them a simple hello. It always feels good when someone remembers you. You could do this via call, text, or email on the basis of what you like and feel comfortable with. Contacting someone for help will be less awkward if you have reached out to them earlier just to chat.

Sometimes a person just pops into your head. Maybe they resemble someone you saw on TV, perhaps you had a dream about them, and maybe you got reminded of a joke they cracked. It could be anything. Whenever this happens, do not hesitate to give them a call and say hi.

5. SHARE KEY LIFE EVENTS

Always keep your contacts updated about the major happenings in your life. Have you moved to a new city or moved house? Did you recently earn a master's degree? Have you changed your email address or phone number? Are you getting married? Announcing a life change to your connections is a good way to reconnect whilst also passing on crucial information. When you make these announcements, you can also include details about your business and career that are worth knowing. This has the capacity to bring new opportunities into your life. It is, however, important that you keep away from words that sound like bragging. Keep balanced as far as the number and frequency of these announcements is concerned. You want to stay in touch, but not at the cost of your associates losing their interest in you.

6. GIVE THEM A RESULTS UPDATE

As you go about your networking activities, you will meet different people and have different kinds of conversations with them. What you speak about might sometimes be vital information such as a life lesson, a piece of advice, or a possible solution to a problem. When you implement the same in your life, be sure to let these people know about it. Tell them how it helped you in making things better. If someone helped you make a connection, tell them what you did with it and how it benefited you. Did that connection lead to the creation of more useful relationships? Did their advice really solve your problem? Always remember to let the person know and thank them for their help. Acknowledging someone's kind gesture always makes them happy. By doing this, you will not only be creating an emotional connection with the person in question but will also be maintaining your relationship with them. If it so happens that the suggestion or advice given by one of your connections doesn't work or works to the negative, do not highlight this in your message to them. Just tell them how grateful you are to receive their words of wisdom, thank them for their time, and stop there. Everyone isn't correct all of the time and your social connections, no matter how experienced or successful they are, are allowed to make mistakes. Remember your larger goal, which is to maintain this relationship. So use this as an opportunity to do just that.

7. INTRODUCE PEOPLE TO YOUR NETWORK

The fact that you are working towards growing your social capital means that you will certainly be associated with a number of networking organizations. You will have a different set of contacts in each one of these different social groups. Try to be a connector, introducing people to one another. If someone in one organization comes to you with the objective of getting to know more people, introduce them to somebody in the other organization you are part of. Connect people and share your connections with your network. This is a great way to keep in touch with all your connections in all the different organizations you are part of. When you introduce a contact to someone, you are helping them develop their social capital; and such an act from your end sends out the word that you are willing to help. As you continue to do more and more people linking, you will become known as a connector in your circle and you will end up developing a stronger network and a richer social resource.

8. SHARE USEFUL INFORMATION

Anybody in the world would only want to build a connection with you if they feel that you could be of some help to them now or in the future. How do you show them that you are indeed valuable? The work you do and the results you achieve will play a significant role in proving your potential to the world, but there is more you can do. When you meet and converse with someone, there is a lot you get to know about them, like their areas of interest, the industry they work in, and what they aspire to achieve in life. Using this information in the right way can work as a kill two birds with one stone kind of situation for you. Wondering how? It's very simple. Find links to articles or websites that contain good quality information on these topics, and share them with the contact in question. If you happen to read a book that you think might interest someone, share a snippet with them. Invites to conferences, business shows, and other networking events are examples of things you can share with your contacts if you feel they might be useful to them. Try to pick something that is related to their company or industry. Little gestures like these show that you are interested and are taking efforts to build a relationship with them. What's more, your contact will feel that you are on top of the news that is important to them and that you understand them and their industry well. This kind of feeling automatically sets the foreground for a beautiful social relationship to blossom and you gain loads of social capital.

So, these were some of the techniques you can use to maintain your relationships and keep your network fresh and strong at all times. Use whichever method you feel most comfortable with. One way to pick the most appropriate method for each of your contacts is to carry out an analysis of your business cards first before diving into the next steps of maintaining and growing the relationship. This simply means that every time you receive a business card, you must classify it. When you receive a business card, you have most likely met that person once, so this is the best time to judge whether or not you wish to continue the relationship with them. Ask yourself the following questions at this stage:

- How was my meeting with this person (in one word)?

- Can this person be of any help to me at any point in my career?

- Do I feel good about having this person in my network?

- What's the first thing that comes to mind when I think about this person, and is that a positive or negative attribute?

If you analyze your answers to the above questions, you will have a fair idea of whether to quit or continue at this stage. If you decide to quit, that's the end of your story with them. If you, however, find this contact good and useful, you must move to the next step of categorizing it. This classification will be based partly on how you feel and partly on how the other person responded. All of your business cards must fall into one of three categories:

9. HOT

This is a contact who is really interested in connecting with you. They have a major interest in you and your business. The contact's business and that of yours are complementary to each other. Complementary businesses are those that operate within the same industry and whose products go well with one another. A mortgage business and a credit repair business would be typical examples. To look at this from a products point of view, think coffee and pastry, hotels and bars, architects and furniture store owners. As a result of the nature of both your businesses, this contact has the potential to turn into an alliance.

10. COOL

This contact falls second on the scale. It could be described as somewhere between good and not ideal. The good part is that the two of you are interested in making a connection, but what isn't so right about this relationship is that your businesses do not complement each other. For example, you are the owner of a financial services business and the other person runs a bakery. This lack of similarity makes you question if this contact could add value to your life, but you do not feel like dismissing the possibility of a relationship straight away.

11. COLD

This is the third and final category. As the name suggests, this is the most uncomfortable contact out of the three. This person is either a competitor or someone who isn't too keen on getting into a relationship.

Once you have your business cards organized, managing and maintaining relationships will become a lot easier. As you continue to meet people, business cards will become a regular thing in your life. Categorizing them as soon as you receive them will ensure you do not miss out on anyone or forget what you liked about them. Digitizing your business card and noting down some key information about the contact would be a good idea to avoid clutter. It will also make it easy for you to refer back to the data if needed. You can do this by using the various applications available, either by scanning your business cards or by manually entering the details into your computer or phone.

How many business cards and connections you have will depend upon your socializing skills and the amount of effort you put into building your network, but Girard's *Law of 250* states that one ordinary person has the power to influence about 250 people. This means that, on average, every person will have about 250 connections in their life. So, what does this indicate? Maintaining your connections well is vital because every single person you meet can influence 250 other people with their opinions and thoughts. All of those 250 people will influence 250 more people. Isn't this wonderful? When one person can have such a huge impact on your life, wouldn't it be an act of mere foolishness on your part to ignore the maintenance aspect of your social capital? This simple yet remarkable law is the product of research conducted by French sociologist and anthropologist Jean Pierre Girard. It was also popularised by Mark Granovetter in his book *The Strength of Weak Ties*.

If you aren't yet convinced that maintaining and growing your social capital is important and can get you to where you want to be in life, here's another piece of research that will blow your mind and will motivate you to start right away. This is called the "six degrees of separation" theory and suggests that any two people in the world are only five or fewer connections apart (Wikipedia 2022). A chain of friends with a maximum of five intermediaries is enough to connect anyone. This means that a friend's friend, their friend's friend, and their friend's friend once again. This is all you have to go through to meet someone and make a connection with them, no matter who they are in the world. In the course of expanding our business, you'll often feel that if you knew Mr. X, you could get advice from him, partner with him, or get your job done. If you apply this in your life, achieving it isn't very difficult.

This theory was first proposed in 1929 by a Hungarian writer named Frigyes Karinthy in a short story called "Chains." In 1967, American sociologist Stanley Milgram used a very interesting experiment to test this theory. So, what did he do? He randomly selected a few people from Kansas and Nebraska to send a package to a stranger in Boston. The participants were provided the name, occupation, and general location of the stranger. Each participant was asked to start by sending the package to the person among their contacts whom they knew on a first-name basis and who, according to them, was most likely to be able to get the package delivered to the target address. The person receiving the package was asked to do the same thing, and everyone subsequently had to follow this up until the package was successfully delivered. Most of the participants expected that around 200 intermediaries would be required to get the job done. In sharp contrast to their expectations, impressive results came out of the study. It only took an average of five to seven intermediaries to deliver the package to a total stranger in another city. If this could be done so easily in the 1960s, when there was no social media or mobile phones, imagine how much easier it would be to achieve this at a time when people have friends and acquaintances all over the globe. If someone asked you to send a package to a stranger in London from New York, you most likely wouldn't have to start with the person in New York. Many people would know somebody residing in a city in Europe or even in London itself. Anything is possible if you set your heart to it. Take the task of growing your social capital as a challenge, write down the names of people you want to connect with, set a target, think out of the box, and break boundaries. You will be amazed to see how quickly you will have gathered a bunch of connections that have the potential to add so much value to your business and life. Every relationship you enter into gives you the opportunity to know many other people and build a massive sphere of influence. This is the millionaire's secret! Below are some tips you can use to form healthy relationships with people:

12. FOCUS ON MUTUAL SUCCESS

Nobody would want to get into a relationship with someone who is self-consumed and only thinks about themselves. It is true that your aim behind building a social network is to derive a benefit from it, but the same holds true for the other person as well, and it is important that you understand this. Think from the point of view of the other party before offering anything. If I was in their place, would this be beneficial to me? If you are asked for a favor or help of any kind, do it with utmost sincerity. Don't attempt to complete it just for the sake of it. For example, if one of your connections comes up to you and asks for contact numbers of good logo designers in town, always provide them with the best. If you think a particular logo designer isn't good enough or isn't nice to work with because of a bad experience you had with them, don't share this contact with them. Care for people and work with utmost loyalty, and the same will come back to you.

13. FOCUS ON RELATIONAL VALUE

This point cannot be stressed enough. When you go out for a networking event or meet someone at a cafe, do not try to sell yourself. Shift your focus away from trying to derive a transactional value from everyone you meet. It is true that benefit is what every person ultimately wants, but look beyond that and focus on building a relationship first. Once you have a good relationship with the person, everything you wish to achieve can be achieved, but if you try to extract profits from someone before establishing a healthy relationship with them, nothing will work for you. Many entrepreneurs and business professionals tend to make this mistake when getting started with their network-building activities. Highly driven and ambitious entrepreneurs are always looking for results in everything they do. It is good to have this mindset in other aspects of your business, but as far as building a relationship is concerned, patience is key. Get into networking with the understanding that all you have to do is give, and you will not be disappointed. Spend as long as it is needed to build trust with your social connections. Try to understand them, their thoughts, and their beliefs. Be a dependable person. If you plan something with someone, do your best to follow through. If you take up responsibility or make a promise to someone, do everything you can to fulfill it. If you practice this consistently, your social connections will slowly but surely begin to trust you. As more and more people begin to feel this way about you, trust will slowly convert into a reputation and this will be immensely beneficial to you in your effort to grow your social capital.

Always remember that no two people are the same. Not being able to celebrate differences is a common stumbling block that comes in the way of healthy relationships. We make the mistake of assuming that everybody will think and act as we do. While it definitely feels good to have a relationship with someone who we think understands our point of view, getting into one with the assumption that it's okay for people to be different will make your networking journey so much easier. Just like any other relationship in your life, your social relationships also need time and attention to blossom. Treat others how you wish to be treated, and success will be all yours.

14. TREAT OTHERS LIKE YOUR FRIENDS AND FAMILY

Authenticity is key when it comes to building healthy business relationships. With everything you do in the process of growing your social capital, try to work towards building trust and credibility with the people in your social circle. Be honest, and have a genuine interest in the person. One kind word is far more powerful than a hundred sugary comments and fake smiles. Try to view everyone as an individual person with their own motives, desires, and thoughts. Make an attempt to establish a deep bond with your connections, and show them through your words and actions how much you genuinely care. Try to add value to the lives of those in your network through your time, resources, connections, and expertise.

Every interaction you have with someone new may not be pleasant. Try to be empathetic because people might forget what you said and what you did, but they will never forget how you made them feel. Give your best to every relationship you enter so that you won't have to regret it even if it doesn't work out the way you want it to.

15. IT'S A PROCESS

Building a relationship is somewhat like building your business. It is a process with different stages. The most effective way to navigate this learning curve successfully is to keep your expectations real all throughout it. It takes time to know people and get along with them, and the best way to create a beautiful healthy social connection for yourself is to give it the time it deserves. The sooner you accept this, the better your journey will be.

Don't rush your relationships. Other people will feel expendable and lose their trust in you. The process of relationship-building is slow but the satisfaction you will get out of it is worth it. You never know which one of your relationships will bring you your big break, so treat them all with the same dedication, respect, and attention.

16. PRIORITIZE QUALITY OVER QUANTITY

We all want to have a huge network of friends and acquaintances, but what's the point if you aren't able to maintain it? Assess your individual personality and circumstances, and make a decision as to how many people you can comfortably manage in your network at one point in time. Interacting and dealing with people is a breeze for some, and a painful chore for others. Where do you stand on this scale? Quality is always more important than quantity when it comes to networking. Having a relationship you cannot maintain is equivalent to not having one.

In this age of social media, friends can be added at the click of a button. Considering how simple this is, we keep overloading our social media accounts with people we barely know anything about. These relationships in most cases have no depth and add no value to your social capital and your life. Aside from randomly friending people on social media, many entrepreneurs also make the mistake of scheduling meetings and connecting with too many people offline. There is no meaning in collecting business cards unless you want to do it for some kind of reward or record. When we join a networking organization, we sometimes get so overwhelmed by the large number of smart and successful people there that we do not want to lose the opportunity to form a relationship with them. You must, however, remember that it's always better to take this slowly. You have joined the organization, and the people you wish to socialize with are going nowhere, so select a few of them to work on at any point in time and take it forward from there.

Here is a simple technique you can use to evaluate how efficient you have been over the years in maintaining your relationships. Browse through your connections on LinkedIn and see how many of them you have spoken to or met face-to-face even once in the past year. How many out of the total connections do you feel are valuable connections to you? Would you give credit to anything coming from them? Do you trust that they will give you sound advice on your business? If yes, how many of them? The answers to these will provide you with a good understanding of how you have done over the past in the sphere of networking. You could also repeat this exercise with your non-social media contacts. Use the conclusion of these little exercises to inform your future networking decisions.

Don't be in the race to emulate someone else's networking story. Only take on as much as you can comfortably manage, and create your own success story.

17. DO SOME RESEARCH

Random interactions with people are one way of growing your network. You go to an event, meet someone, and begin a relationship. This, however, is never sufficient if you want to grow your social capital quickly. You will need to ask people to introduce you to other people or you will need to find the kind of people you want to have a relationship with on your own. One thing to remember when indulging in targeted networking is to try and know as much as possible about the person before you actually plan a meeting with them. We are all different individuals, and so are our likes and preferences. The purpose of the first meeting is often an opportunity to assess whether or not you wish to move on with this relationship. So, carrying out some research about the contact beforehand will help you avoid unproductive meetings. Here are some things you should attempt to find out through your research:

- Some basic details about the person, like who they are, where they live, their educational qualification, which school/university they completed their graduation and post-graduation from, etc.

- If the person is an entrepreneur, what is their business all about? Have a look at their website and social media pages, both personal and professional.

- Try to learn about their career graph from whatever is available about them online. You could even ask the person who introduced you to them to provide you with some details.

- Do you think you will be able to add value to their life? If yes, how?

Networking is more about focusing on giving rather than receiving as discussed earlier, but if your accomplishments and circumstances do not allow for you to contribute positively to someone else's business or life, such a relationship would have no meaning and wouldn't last even if initiated. Being able to add value might seem like a very easy thing to do, but it actually isn't. No matter how confident you feel about your ability to do so, try to perform a realistic fact check about this and list out at least a couple of ways in which you plan to do it. Use all the data you collected to assess if a relationship with this person is what you want or not. This will not only make you feel more confident but will also help to avoid unnecessary waste of time and energy. Why take on the hassle of meeting up when you know this isn't going to help either of you?

Your social capital is more valuable than you know, and building it can be made simple with just a little bit of planning and hard work. Socializing has been a part of human existence for ages, so most of us don't feel the need to attach too much importance to it. We make the mistake of thinking that it will just happen. This kind of thinking and the lack of understanding prevents us from engaging in any sort of preparation or planning in this regard. We, therefore, end up achieving nothing great from a goldmine that has the ability to transform our lives. So, try to avoid these pitfalls by practicing the tips discussed above, and make the magic of social capital that people talk about real for you.

In the next chapter, you will learn about some of the resources available out there that you can use to maximize your chances of achieving great social capital.

CHAPTER FIVE:
. . . .

POPULAR NETWORKING RESOURCES

You might be wondering: "Ok, I have a good understanding of why I should network, how to build my social capital, how and why to work on maintaining it, and all of that. But what's the easiest way to start? I'm too worked up to research. Which are those networking groups that will give me the biggest bank for my buck?"

There are so many options out there that it is easy to be overwhelmed. Likewise, you may choose an avenue that is not a good fit for your personality. But there is no need for that because we're here for you.

This chapter will give you all the answers. Let me first give you a quick rundown of the major kinds of business networking groups you will find out there, and we will then move on to the specifics. There are basically five major types of networking groups, and the organizations you see will usually fall within one of these. Below is a brief overview of each of them.

1. CASUAL NETWORKING GROUPS

These are general business groups that aim to connect people from a wide variety of professions. Meetings are held in an informal style and usually take place once every month. What basically happens at such networking events is that people simply mingle with one another with the objective of making connections. Guest speakers are sometimes invited to discuss business-related subjects with members, and local business, community affairs, and legislation serve as conversation starters to facilitate relationship forming and bonding. Natural, unplanned, and unrestricted networking is the central theme around which these meetings are based. There are no stringent joining rules or entry requirements. Your local Chamber of Commerce is a classic example of a casual contact network. If you are someone who prefers casual and fun ways of socializing as opposed to the more structured and focused methods, and you prefer to meet as large a number of people as possible at every event, then this kind of networking is right for you.

There are, however, two sides to every coin. While casual contact networking will offer you the opportunity to meet a lot of people and give you enormous exposure, converting these relationships into real business ones is not easy. Despite the fact that there are no specific rules about which kinds of business professionals and entrepreneurs can join these organizations and which ones cannot, not every kind of entrepreneur will be able to derive benefits from this type of networking. Trust is an essential ingredient for business relationships to flourish, and a casual networking environment is not best suited to enable this to happen. If your purpose of socializing is to get referrals for your business, this method wouldn't be the ideal choice because networks of this kind are not primarily tailored to help with this. If you are into a business that doesn't require you to develop a deep level of trust and if your sales cycles are relatively short, like in retail for example, then casual contact networks could work well for your enterprise.

2. STRONG CONTACT NETWORKS

This is a more focused method of networking and as the name suggests, it helps you to build strong relationships with the people you meet. The main aim of such a network is to help you get referrals for your business. They are also called strong contact referral groups due to this reason. Members typically meet once every week over lunch or breakfast, but the strength of these meetings is relatively small. As opposed to casual contact networks, you wouldn't be interacting with hundreds of people here. Membership in such groups is limited to one member per profession or specialty. Strong contact networks can provide you with focused opportunities to build long-term relationships with people. It's a great platform to develop your referral marketing campaigns. All of the people you interact with at these events will in a sense serve as your marketing and sales team, carrying your business card with them wherever they go. Strong contact networking groups can help you build powerful invaluable connections, provided you find the time to attend all of their scheduled events. Investing time is essential because the process of knowing and understanding the businesses of others is a lengthy one and cannot be completed in a single meet-up. Regular attendance is also important in order to build a rapport with the other members of your group.

Networking is about reciprocity, and strong contact networks are especially stringent when it comes to this aspect of socializing. As hard as you work to get referrals for your own business, you will need to put in the effort to bring in referrals for the other members of your group as well. You will, therefore, need to feel comfortable attending events, finding prospects, and making connections with the people from whom you think your group members will benefit. Most good and reputed strong contact networks track the performance of their members on a regular basis, and do not appreciate the participation of those who cannot contribute or add value to the network. If your performance isn't satisfactory, you will either be asked to leave or referrals will stop coming your way. Stringency in this regard can sometimes feel suffocating and could also appear as a disadvantage or put you off, but it will only bring you profits and success in the long run.

3. COMMUNITY SERVICE CLUBS

These organizations are slightly different from the kinds discussed above. The main objective here is service to the community. These networks revolve around the fundamental principle that if you voluntarily serve the community in whichever way you can, you will accumulate social capital that will bring you material benefits in the long run. You will find a large number of such groups out there, each supporting a different cause, and you can join the ones you feel most passionate about. Some entrepreneurs make the mistake

of joining these organizations in the hope of deriving a direct business benefit and end up disappointed. If you are someone who is willing to contribute
rather than benefit from the beginning, this category of networking groups
would be right for you.

4. PROFESSIONAL ASSOCIATIONS

These groups are targeted at people from a specific industry or profession.
For example, you will find professional groups for bankers, lawyers, design
companies, the health sector, architecture, accounting, etc. The main aim of
these groups is to exchange information and ideas among members. Since
these are specific groups targeted at specific types of people, you wouldn't
have a great number of options to choose from. Your goal when joining
these groups should be to tap into clients or target markets. A good idea to
find a professional association that is most appropriate for you would be to
ask your clients or customers which groups they are part of and join those.
Many groups limit membership to those people that have specific industry
credentials and often do not encourage the participation of vendors. It is
important you do your research before selecting one for yourself. A good
way to stand out in such associations would be to help members without
selling your services. For instance, if you are an entrepreneur running a
social media consulting business, you can offer to manage the Facebook
and Instagram pages of the organization as a voluntary service from your
end. This will automatically shine a light on your expertise, thereby bringing
opportunities your way.

So, these are some of the major types of networking groups you will
find. As more and more people are beginning to take the path of entrepreneurship, the number of networking organizations and groups being operated and even newly incorporated to help these change-makers to make a
mark on the markets is at an all-time high. Below is a list of some popular
groups to simplify your research and help you make the right choice.

5. NETWORK LEAD EXCHANGE (NLX)

This is a US-based network of businesses established to help entrepreneurs get referrals for their ventures. They have 60 chapters all across the country and provide member businesses the opportunity to build relationships with other members, especially those within their own chapter. Since the intent here is to help members get referrals, a certain amount of money is paid in the form of a commission to those making the referral. In order to join this organization, your first step would be to locate the chapter that is nearest to you. You will then be required to create a profile on the platform, and your networking journey with Network Lead Exchange begins. In case there isn't a chapter in your area, you also have the option of starting one. NLX is known for the high quality of the referrals they provide. This group caters to all kinds of businesses and all types of entrepreneurs. There are no commitments to attend meetings, and you are free to network when you want, where you want, and with whomever you want. Everything on the platform, including the handling of commissions, is very simple and user-friendly. If you are looking for a networking group that is locally focused, then NLX would be the perfect choice for you.

6. HAPPY NEIGHBORHOOD PROJECT (HNP)

This is touted as a happy place for business leaders where they can build relationships, get referrals and collaborate with like-minded people from the corporate world. This networking group was formed in 2020 and provides a platform for people around the world to mingle online through various events. They host multicultural meetings where people from different backgrounds can meet and bond with one another, and they also have events specifically targeted at minority groups such as Asian, black, and Hispanic communities. The HNP website has a complete list of meeting options available to you, which you can choose from based on your interests and preferences. You do not need to satisfy any entry requirements to join this organization. They have two membership options, a basic plan and a premium one. Both of these are paid, and prices range from $50 to $100 a month.

7. NATIONAL ASSOCIATION FOR THE SELF-EMPLOYED (NASE)

Founded in 1981, this is another non-profit organization that provides day-to-day support to entrepreneurs. They can provide you with access to resources that are usually only available to large corporations. It is the largest non-profit organization of its kind if you are looking for legal support, funding, or direct access to experts to get their perspective on business trends. The NASE is the place for you. They have experts from various fields such as finance, accounting, database management, information technology, healthcare, marketing, real estate, sales tax, social media, business filings, and insurance. The members of this organization also get access to a learning center consisting of a huge bank of articles, guides, and more. If you opt for their monthly newsletter, you can receive useful tips on how to more effectively manage your business, and can also stay updated about the latest happenings in the world of business. Entrepreneurs have a number of membership plan options to choose from, all of which are paid.

8. SOCIAL ENTERPRISE ALLIANCE (SEA)

This organization is targeted at social entrepreneurs and has a growing network of members across 39 states and 10+ chapters in the US. They have a combination of both free and paid resources to help social enterprises expand their business and the scope of their impact. They do so by creating awareness about the planet and providing access to resources, thereby empowering businesses to become sustainable. The SEA is an accredited social enterprise and is, therefore, committed to working in support of the planet and people in general over and above shareholder gains. They believe that businesses should make profits whilst protecting and improving the environment, and strive to help entrepreneurs who share a similar vision to grow their revenue.

9. YOUNG ENTREPRENEUR COUNCIL (YEC)

This is a community of passionate entrepreneurs based in the US. It is an invitation-only association that can be joined by entrepreneurs that meet the following criteria: are 45 years old or younger; are the founder, co-founder, owner, or co-owner of a business; the business must have at least $1 million in revenue or funding. This is another organization that was created by entrepreneurs to help other entrepreneurs overcome the challenges and trials of running a business. The members of this organization are provided access to concierge-level services, business resources, and media exposure. The main aim of this organization is to establish meaningful connections among entrepreneurs to make their journey easier and more enjoyable. You will have the opportunity to meet other like-minded business leaders and use their support and guidance to overcome your challenges and reach your business goals. If you choose to join, you will be provided access to an online interface where you can connect with, send direct messages to, and interact with other members. Other services available to members include access to support with content created exclusively for you, one on one business and executive coaching, premium access to a personal coach who can help you reach your milestones, face-to-face events in different parts of the country, annual retreat to a private mountain, and vacation benefits, such as transportation and hotels to make your travels memorable. It should, however, be noted that despite all the benefits, you can derive from joining this organization, getting past the entry barrier isn't easy. This is a very selective organization that focuses on quality over quantity as far as membership is concerned. There are two ways to join the Young Entrepreneur Council. The first method is by filling up the form found on their website. If you fit the criteria mentioned above, just fill in the form and the YEC team will get in touch with you. The second and easier option is by getting a referral. If you know an existing member of YEC, schedule a meeting with them and request them to refer you to the board. YEC includes members from a variety of industries and has been helping entrepreneurs get media coverage, raise funds, and build connections for over a decade now.

10. YOUNG PRESIDENTS ORGANIZATION (YPO)

This is the largest community of CEOs in the world, with members from over 130 countries. What began as a group of 20 chief executives in 1950 has now grown to become a massive global network of around 30,000 members. This global community aims to support leaders in improving businesses and making the world a better place. You will need to meet the following membership requirements if you wish to join this organization: you should be under the age of 45; you must be the chief executive officer, chairperson, managing director, managing partner, or hold any other equivalent position in your organization; you must have 50 full-time employees or at least a minimum of 15+ full-time employees in your organization; your annual employee compensation must be $2 million at the least; your business must meet the minimum revenue threshold which is $13 million plus for sales, manufacturing, and service, $10 million plus for agency businesses, and over $260 million for financial institutions. You will need to complete a membership application form on the YPO website. Each submission is evaluated on the basis of the past achievements of the applicant and their potential for leadership success.

11. VISTAGE

This is the world's largest coaching network that helps entrepreneurs overcome their business-related challenges and make decisions. Its target members are the CEOs, owners, and top-level executives of small and mid-size businesses. The business community has been benefiting from its services for the past 60 years. Vistage members represent a variety of different industries, sectors, and nationalities. They have created a huge number of success stories by assisting businesses in turning around their valuations from a mere zero dollars to several millions of dollars. The members of this organization were able to report growth in every aspect of their business at challenging times in history when the rest of their industry was experiencing a decline. For instance, during the pandemic of 2020, the members of this organization saw a 4.6% increase in revenue as opposed to the 4.7% fall that their comparable non-member businesses faced over the same period. Confidential peer advisory groups consisting of around 12 to 16 local business owners from non-competing industries to facilitate discussion, coaching sessions with access to a trustworthy and qualified executive coach, and one-to-one mentoring are at the heart of their service offering. Over 27,000 leaders from 26 countries make up the Vistage community. This network has served as a troubleshooter for more than 100,000 business professionals so far. If you are looking to grow your company faster and maximize your impact as a leader, Vistage is the right choice for you. In order to join this organization, you will need to complete the application form on their website. One day every month for meetings is all you will have to set aside if you choose to become a member.

12. GLOBAL ENTREPRENEURSHIP NETWORK (GEN)

Want to start or scale up your business? The Global Entrepreneurship Network can make the process easier for you. This organization, which operates in around 200 countries of the world, aims to connect entrepreneurs, investors, researchers, policymakers, and entrepreneur support organizations from across borders to foster collaboration. It has a number of programs to support and facilitate learning, accelerate innovation, and promote economic growth. All of their programs are relevant and up-to-date and are specially tailored to every country on matters such as the size of the economy and how mature it is, language, culture, geography, and more. Not every country has a well-developed entrepreneurial ecosystem like the one you can find in Silicon Valley, and GEN helps to solve this problem by understanding, supporting, and assisting entrepreneurs. They help to break down silos by hosting numerous live and virtual global events. Its regular start-up competitions and awards also help to encourage and motivate entrepreneurs while also keeping their enthusiasm and entrepreneurial spirit alive.

13. CLUB HOUSE

This networking resource is the latest craze in the entrepreneurial world. It is an audio-based mobile application that connects entrepreneurs, influencers, musicians, executives, and artists. Membership in this organization provides you access to a virtual room where you can meet all the top talent.

This fascinating app has a lot of content and can provide you with the opportunity to listen to and chat with people you otherwise wouldn't have access to. From learning useful stuff such as digital marketing to speaking with the president of Shopify, you can do it all here. This app is quite a new addition to the networking universe. When it first started, it made huge waves because it was an invitation-only app with interesting and useful features for entrepreneurs. Recently, the app has become open to anyone wanting to join. All you need to do is download it and complete the initial registration procedures. The ability to leave a room whenever you want and enter whenever you like gives members great flexibility. Since all interactions are voice-only, there is no hassle of dressing up or preparing your home for a video recording. Although this is an online networking platform, you as a member are not entirely anonymous. You can make comments and express your opinion in your own voice, thereby keeping your individuality alive. It is very convenient as there are no commitments with regard to membership. You can join and leave whenever you like. You also do not require any specialized production capabilities to start a room or initiate a conversation. All in all, Club House provides quality networking opportunities in a very easy and user-friendly format, so there are literally no excuses for not attending events.

14. EXECUTIVE SUITE

This is another online networking group that you can access from the comfort of your home or office. It is a private LinkedIn group for senior-level professionals and includes over 350,000 members. The best part is it's completely free. You can get access to a large number of learning resources, such as online sessions led by accomplished CEOs, B-school professors, and business strategists. If you are in the process of establishing your business or working towards expanding it, this could be a great place for you to learn and get advice. Since this is an online group, you can expect to have members from all around the globe, and as a result, ideas and perspectives from a wide variety of culturally diverse people. Aside from learning, you will get to make connections with people from different cultures, which in turn can help you expand your social capital beyond geographical border.

15. WOMEN'S BUSINESS ENTERPRISE NATIONAL COUNCIL (WBENC)

Are you a female entrepreneur? If so, this networking group is for you. WBENC is a nonprofit organization aimed at helping women in business. You will need to start by getting your enterprise certified. This is a thorough process that requires you to meet certain eligibility criteria. Your business must be at least 51% owned, controlled, operated, and managed by a woman. The certification process also includes a detailed review of your documentation and a site visit. Successful completion of these steps will give you a WBENC certification which is considered to be the gold standard of business certifications for women-owned enterprises. This certification could be a great marketing tool for your business, and can open the door of opportunities for you. Some of the benefits you can expect to receive include opportunities to carry out business with corporate and government members; access to procurement executives, mentoring facilities, and executive learning courses; access to a wide variety of business development tools; a number of coaching programs, awards, and scholarships; targeted business opportunities and increased visibility for your enterprise; resources to help you grow your venture; and access to a vast network of like-minded individuals to support and encourage you and other women entrepreneurs like you.

16. LETIP

This is the oldest networking organization in the US. It provides its members with the opportunity to socialize with one another in a competition-free environment. At LeTip, you will be able to build lasting relationships with leaders within your industry as well as outside it. This organization is different from other networking groups in that it does not invite outside speakers to its events. Members are given the chance to speak about their business in a pitch every week and also in a 10-minute presentation each month. This way, you will be able to get to know about the businesses of all of your fellow members, enabling you to take advantage of opportunities and also create them for yourself. As the name suggests, LeTip is about exchanging tips with each other, and the diverse pool of members can make this exchange really useful. This is quite a well-known organization and a trusted one too, so finding a chapter near you won't be difficult. Another interesting feature of this networking organization is that its membership can be passed from one generation to the next. So, it can in essence become a family organization for small and medium-sized businesses looking for a low-cost, yet highly beneficial method of growing their social capital.

17. WECONNECT INTERNATIONAL

This is another networking organization targeted at women entrepreneurs. The aim here is to connect all kinds of women in business to the rest of the world in order to enable them to raise funds and grow their venture. This organization aspires to create a world in which women have the same opportunities as men. Whether it is finding solutions to problems, expanding their business beyond boundaries or anything else in between, Weconnect International has been working to provide women entrepreneurs equal access to every kind of resource they might need to fulfill their entrepreneurial dream. Joining this organization is easy. There aren't too many stringent entry requirements. You will, however, be required to fill in a questionnaire and complete a member registration process on their website. Weconnect International, like WBENC, serves as a certification body for women-owned businesses. A WBE certification, as it is called, is a symbol of trust and reliability, making a business stand out to entrepreneurs all over the world. This certification option is available to businesses in a total of 50 countries. Every enterprise must satisfy four criteria to be able to get the Weconnect International seal of certification. Criteria include ownership, management, control, and independence. Businesses wanting to join must be at least 51% owned and managed by one or more women. The global verification status you will receive as a result of this certification is highly prestigious and beneficial. Access to an international network of women entrepreneurs, an academy of high-quality learning resources, and a host of trade and business opportunities are just a few of the many pluses of joining Weconnect.

18. CHAMBER OF COMMERCE

This is one of the most popular networking organizations among entrepreneurs in most countries of the world. If you are new at networking, your local Chamber of Commerce is a great place to start. It can help you form connections within your own community. As the owner of a small business, you can expect to get help with foundational training and professional development for yourself and your enterprise. You will also have access to resources to help grow and expand your venture. While the services provided and the nature of the events hosted by this organization might vary between chapters, the opportunity to build connections is a sure benefit of joining it. Many chapters also invite guest speakers from time to time and provide mentorship facilities to help entrepreneurs gain knowledge and advice from the more experienced and successful leaders in the business world. The US Chamber of Commerce is the largest business organization in the world, consisting of a large number of members and chapters, so finding a chapter near you won't be difficult. You must, however, remember that the Chamber of Commerce is a casual contact network and you will have to put in a lot of hard work to get referrals for your business through it. One way to easily build a number of useful connections with very little time commitment is to become a Chamber Ambassador. Sitting on committees is a great way to stay in the limelight and meet new people.

19. BUSINESS NETWORK INTERNATIONAL (BNI)

This is the world's largest business referral organization with over 10,000 chapters and 290,000 members. If you're looking for client referrals, this is the place to be in. This organization also has an online portal where members can connect with other business leaders from around the globe. BNI has a dedicated team at the regional as well as the global level to provide technical support to members and help them grow. This organization encourages equality and non-discrimination. As a result of this, members are selected from different professional backgrounds irrespective of race, color, income levels, disability, age, religion, and sexual orientation. If you wish to become a part of this incredibly successful organization, your first step would be to look for a chapter close to you. Finding a chapter is very easy. Just use the "find a chapter map" feature on the website, and you can get this done in no time. Once you have found one, get in touch with them and enquire about their meeting schedule. You cannot straightaway become a member of Business Network International. You will have to attend one meeting as a visitor and share details about your business, clients, and how you can help others and the organization grow. You will also need to fill in an application form and go through an interview with the leadership team. If the members believe that your inclusion could add value to the organization, you will be sent an invitation to join. The members of BNI are assigned a mentor who will help them grow both professionally, whilst making the best use of the resources provided by the organization.

20. THE AMERICAN MARKETING ASSOCIATION (AMA)

Whether you work in the field of marketing or not, this is a great organization to be a part of. Marketing is an essential part of every entrepreneur's life. No matter which stage your business is in, knowing how to effectively market your products/services is key to your success in business. The American Marketing Association can provide you with all the resources you need to sharpen your marketing skills and expand your knowledge in the subject. Founded in 1937, this organization has been helping marketing professionals for over 80 years. It publishes a number of journals and handbooks on various aspects of marketing such as research, strategies, best practices, and educational resources. Your local AMA chapter could be a great place for you to boost your knowledge, advance your career, and make connections with entrepreneurs and marketing professionals in your area. You can also receive career coaching and exclusive access to a number of marketing-related webcasts and blogs. The more knowledge you have about marketing, the farther you can go in business. In the process of learning how to market your products, you will gain a deep understanding of the subject itself, and this knowledge could be greatly beneficial to you in your social capital-building efforts. After all, a major part of networking is knowing how to market yourself and your business, isn't it?

21. ROTARY CLUB INTERNATIONAL

This is a global organization that brings business professionals around the world together with the objective of giving back to the community. If you like the idea of building your social capital whilst serving the community, then this organization is the right fit for you. Rotary has been around for over 115 years. What started as a small entity in Illinois, United States, has grown by leaps and bounds, and now has chapters all across the world. Meetings are periodically held to help people connect and to create lasting change in the world. Giving their time to Rotary for a good cause has helped many entrepreneurs build meaningful relationships and advance their careers. So how do you become a member of this well-known organization? Memberships are accepted at Rotary Club International by invitation only. You will be required to fill up a form on the basis of which your membership in the organization will be determined. This form is quite straightforward and generally includes questions about yourself and your interests. Getting past this stage and becoming a member of the club is not very difficult. The only criteria you are required to fulfill in order to become a member of Rotary is that you should be willing to give back to the community. One of the most popular events of the club is the Rotary Convention, which sees members from 130 countries come together to bond with each other and help the community. The club also has events in which members are required to use their professional skills to benefit society at large.

22. NETWORK AFTER WORK (NAW)

This is a community of entrepreneurs, business professionals, executives, and thought leaders established to help its members develop meaningful and long-lasting relationships. Set up 10 years ago, this organization uses a combination of both online as well as offline methods to accomplish its objectives. On the online front, NAW enables its members to interact with other like-minded individuals by creating an account on their platform and mingling with the others on it, social media style. Aside from these virtual meet-ups and workshops, members also have the opportunity to meet in person at the various face-to-face events organized by the club. Becoming a member of NAW is easy both as a process as well as on the pocket. The amount of $39 per year is all you have to spend to become a member and unlock all the benefits that come with it.

23. SOCIAL CALENDARS

These are online directories that contain information about networking events happening around you. They include details about music festivals, cultural events, and traditional networking events as well. One popular online directory is Meetup. With the help of this platform, you can look for events based on your interest and the kind of people you want to mingle with. Based on your location, you can expect to participate in activities such as visiting a museum, trying out food, attending music festivals, or going on a brewery or winery tour. Meetup has been around for over 20 years and has been helping people build new connections, make friends, and explore the world by stepping out of their comfort zone. You can find a number of different groups on this platform, and join the ones you like the most. For example, if you wish to expand your knowledge or sharpen your skills, you could join career groups. These groups can help you learn a new language, test a prototype, pitch your product to investors, or develop a new skill whilst building your social capital along the way. If you like the idea of networking while doing something you love, then creativity groups could be the right choice for you. Whether you like to create art, design something, start a podcast, write a story or a poem, make music, or engage in any other creative activity, you are sure to find people with similar interests and skill sets to keep you company. There are two ways in which you can join Meetup. The first is by selecting a group of your choice and joining it straight away, and the second option is to create your own group. It's usually quite easy to find something you love to do on this platform and if you don't, you always have the second option. There are more than 200,000 meet-up groups in over 180 countries, and about 24 million people have signed up on the platform. You are sure to find a group around you no matter where in the world you live. Another online directory that is quite popular is Eventbrite. This platform is quite similar to Meetup and provides similar services and opportunities to help you accomplish your networking goals. Unlike other networking organizations, Meetup doesn't have a fixed membership fee. Those organizing event groups need to pay a certain amount of money to use the platform. Each group can then decide how to divide this cost among its members. This form of networking is quite easy and informal. It doesn't require its members to comply with many stringent rules or satisfy any long list of entry requirements. Can there be anything better than having fun while accumulating the most valuable asset in the world for yourself?

24. MY OPPORTUNITY

This is a networking community for business professionals and job seekers that is open to everyone around the world. It was founded in 2014 and boasts a total membership count of around 6 million. Joining this group is easy. Just create a profile for yourself on their website or mobile app, and you are done. They have two membership options to choose from, a basic free plan and a paid premium plan. Both of these can provide millions of business opportunities for your enterprise. With My Opportunity, you will be able to stay connected to the people and industries that can help you grow your business and achieve your goals. You will also have the opportunity to turbocharge your sales lead generation by connecting with your target market via their online portal, and creating brand awareness for your business with the help of the My Opportunity advertising platform. This organization makes hiring talented professionals so much easier and quicker through their AI match facility, which helps to link the right candidates with the right recruiters.

25. DIY NETWORKS

Finally, if none of the above work for you and your business, there is always the option of creating your own networking group. This will allow you greater freedom and control with regard to the kind of organizations and entrepreneurs you want to connect with as opposed to other networking groups where your options are limited to the people attending the event. You can form your own rules and host your own events. This is a great way for service businesses to form connections within their local community. Like you are your own boss for your business, you will be the master of your networking universe as well if you choose to walk the DIY path to build your social capital.

Building your social capital is a fast track to success, but the process of doing it doesn't have to be formal all of the time. All of the networking organizations discussed above could really help you form connections, acquire knowledge and skills, receive advice, and build strategic alliances with a whole lot of new people from different walks of life. Most of these organizations are not more than a hundred years old. In fact, many of them in this list have been established in the last 50 years or so. So, does this mean that networking is a new concept? Didn't our forefathers understand the value of social capital? They surely did. Although this understanding didn't stem from any research or published theories, the people who lived in the centuries before us also socialized with one another. They didn't have the internet or telephone to communicate with one another. Traveling from one city to another took days, and making your way from country to country took several months. People couldn't send messages to their friends as quickly as we do via WhatsApp and text today. So what does all of this indicate? Networking can be done anywhere and in any way, both with and without the use of modern methods.

When hunters met one another to discuss the best places to hunt in the forest, they were networking. When communities organized carnivals on their local fairgrounds, they were creating an opportunity for their members to socialize. Meeting under a tree in the evenings for a chat, visiting the homes of their neighbors and friends, congregating at church every Sunday, engaging in activities such as fishing and picnicking with neighbors, and simply helping each other in every little and large activity are examples of past socializing. These activities enabled the people of that era to create strong, bonded relationships as well as casual connections with the people in their cities and the surrounding areas. All of these activities they did are still prevalent in our lives today, so why can't we practice them more frequently and use them to build our social capital? The centuries before ours witnessed the greatest number of inventions in the whole of history. If this level of social engagement was enough to create so many miraculous things then, can the same not benefit us today? If they could do it so successfully, why can't we? The best way to be successful in networking is to use a combination of the past as well as the present. Create for yourself a perfect mix of both traditional and modern methods of socializing, and this formula could help you soar higher and higher in your career. There is a reason why they say, "Old is gold." So, use it to add a dash of glamor to your networking story.

CHAPTER SIX:

....

PREPARING YOURSELF FOR NETWORKING

Every entrepreneur is a unique personality in their own right. While some are social butterflies, happy among people, a few of them are more comfortable being in their own cocoon. While every individual has a good chance of attaining success as an entrepreneur, there are some traits and habits that can put you at an advantage over others. Nobody is born perfect. We all need some polishing and sharpening to be able to socialize effectively. The good news, however, is that social skills aren't hard to master, and with an adequate amount of perseverance, patience, and practice, all of which you already possess as an entrepreneur, inculcating new habits and breaking those that aren't benefiting you isn't too difficult either. The first step, though, is to be mindful of your own strengths and weaknesses, and aware of those characteristics and habits that could make you an expert at networking. You will only be able to fill a gap if you know one exists, and knowing which facets of your personality need improvement isn't rocket science. A good read through the below list can also help enlighten you about the same.

1. BE AN ACTIVE LISTENER AND ASK THE RIGHT QUESTIONS

This is a simple yet the most important aspect of effective socializing. Listening isn't the same as hearing. How much you can gain from a conversation with a social connection is directly related to how attentively you are able to listen when speaking to them. Imagine yourself talking to a prospective client at a networking event. You are physically sitting across the table from this person, but your eyes are busy scanning who's doing what in the room you are in or checking the notifications flashing on your phone. What would the outcome of such a discussion be? Not only will the opposite party feel offended, but they will also relay this negative impression of you to everyone they meet. This behavior is not a conscious one and is on many occasions a result of nervousness. Think about a time when you met someone new. Do you, on reflection, feel that you didn't pay as much attention as you should have? If yes, this is something you must work on. When you meet someone and start a conversation with them, make sure your entire attention is on the person and what they have to say. Listen attentively to them and ask appropriate questions when necessary. Your aim should be to get a thorough understanding of the conversation. Just nodding occasionally and not speaking much is equivalent to a lost opportunity. You worked hard to arrange a meeting with this person who has the potential to help you grow and realize your dreams, but you will only be able to evaluate how you can achieve this if you listen carefully, process the information, and ask the right questions.

Avoid the temptation to ask too many questions just to make the speaker feel that you are paying attention. Questions should only be asked when you need clarification or a further explanation about something that has been said. Doing otherwise will not serve you well and will not give the impression you want the person you are speaking with to have about you. Here are some tips to help you ask the right questions in the right way:

- Don't go off-topic.

- Ask positive questions.

- Don't offend the opposite person by comparing them to others.

- Be empathetic and authentic.

- Don't ask too many questions. Keep the balance.

Listening well and asking questions are two of the most important skills you will need to have if you wish to build your social capital. They can impress your contacts much more than your strongest business figures can ever do. Good listening is a sign of respect, and asking thoughtful questions shows that you are sincere. Both of these traits can contribute to making you come across as a trustworthy person. If you want people to get interested in you and your business, you will need to learn to listen more than you talk. So how do you become a good listener? Here are some actions you can take:

- Try to maintain eye contact at all times.

- Do not fidget with your hair or clothing or any other object around you.

- Do not change your sitting or standing position too often, i.e., sitting back and moving forward on your chair or shifting your weight from one foot to the other when standing.

- Try not to look at your phone each time the message tone beeps.

- Do not interrupt the opposite person to make your point or express your opinion; wait for them to finish, and then begin speaking.

- Respond by repeating at least one important point your contact made. For example, if John said that he is excited about the launch of his new brand of shoes, ask him when this line is likely to be launched. Always make it a point to structure this return comment in the form of a question.

Doing any of the above the other way around will make the person feel that you are not interested or are just bored talking to them. You should always try to make the person with whom you are working to build a connection feel good about themselves. Science suggests that when someone feels good about themselves in a conversation with you, they tend to attribute that positive emotion to you and feel good about you as a result. Listening to people and getting them to talk about their accomplishments makes them feel valued and elevates their self-image, thereby making them like themselves and you. Isn't it amazing to see how much a simple act of listening attentively can do for you?

2. COMMUNICATE WELL

This is another very important networking skill every business owner must possess. You might be the most successful entrepreneur in your area, but at the end of the day, it is how you speak and what you say to the people you meet that matters. Whether you are intelligent, smart, talented, skillful, insightful, or anything else have no meaning if you aren't able to communicate it across to the people you socialize with. When you attend a networking event, be mindful of how you talk and respond to your connections. Pay attention to the language you use and your tone of voice. Visualize yourself through the lens of the other person. Does all of what you do and say seem appealing and attractive? Would you be drawn toward speaking to a person like you? If you find it difficult to perform this analysis during an event, try recording one of your meetings. Listen to the recording later, analyze and evaluate your responses, and try to figure out what went wrong and what you did well. Your urgency to speak over others could also sometimes be off-putting. The purpose of communication is to convey your point clearly. Listen attentively to yourself and find out if you were able to do this or not.

A conversation that is simple and straightforward is often very easy to handle. You do not need to put in much effort to feel at ease and communicate freely. It would, however, be unrealistic to expect every interaction to go well. You will have to respond effectively to negative statements, sarcastic comments, conflicting viewpoints, and a lot more. Observe yourself and analyze how good you are at doing this. If you find it hard to judge your own self, you could always ask a friend or a well-wisher for their opinions and feedback. Listening to YouTube videos on the subject of effective communication and podcasts of business discussions could be a great way to learn and sharpen your communication skills. When you go to a networking event, try to observe how other entrepreneurs and business leaders communicate. Evaluate what is good and bad about their style, and use this insight to modify and improve your approach. Ultimately, good communication is all about practice. As you do more of it, you will naturally get better at the skill.

3. NON-VERBAL COMMUNICATION

Communication doesn't stop with the words you speak. Everything about you other than what you speak verbally also conveys a message. This includes your body language, the way you sit, how you walk, the way you dress, your position towards the other person, your facial expression, and so on. Take a moment to think about this. Whom are you more likely to strike a conversation with, a person with hunched shoulders and a stiff upper lip, or someone who radiates positivity and confidence? Surely the latter. In order to put your best foot forward, it is important that you prepare yourself adequately before every networking event. Spend a while thinking about how the event is likely to be. Is it a conference room with a large number of attendees or an outdoor location with only a few executives? Try to visualize the event and yourself in it. What kind of people will you be meeting? What are some of the likely questions you may be asked? How will you conduct yourself during that time? It's quite normal to feel nervous or even anxious when meeting somebody new, so some amount of prior mental preparation will really help you navigate the whole scenario with ease. Below are some pointers you must remember and follow every time you go out to socialize:

- Always have a smile on your face, no matter how crappy your day was.

- Make sure the clothes you choose to wear are clean, well-fitted, and well-ironed. Pick an outfit that will bring out the best in you and make you stand out from the crowd. You don't have to stick to the standard greys, blues, and blacks. It's perfectly alright to add some color to keep the fun element alive. However, if there is a theme or dress code, try your best to follow it. You do not want to leave an impression that you are unprofessional or inappropriately dressed. No matter what you decide to wear, make sure to choose something you look good in and keep your individuality alive.

- Look and smell fresh. Nobody, including you, would be interested in interacting with a person who is on the verge of dozing off into a deep slumber or smelling bad.

- Whether you're seated or standing or walking about, always maintain an erect posture. Always stand or sit straight with your shoulders back and head held up. This reflects confidence and positivity.

- Use your eyebrows to show your reaction to comments. The point here is to look interested and engaged.

- Try to use effective hand gestures where appropriate. They can increase the value of what you're saying. Be careful not to overdo this though.

- Don't cross your arms. This is often considered to be a sign of defensiveness and can make others feel that you are not open to conversation.

- It isn't necessary for you to pose a certain way while conversing with people. There is nothing called "the magic pose" that can show you off as more confident and attractive, not even the hands on the hip pose that is touted by many as the "power pose." All you should strive for is being your best self.

- Don't make people feel uncomfortable by standing too close to them. An arm's length away is the best distance to keep. This is particularly important to keep in mind when you are meeting somebody of the opposite gender.

- Pay attention to your tone of voice and sound volume. You should be audible. People shouldn't have to struggle to hear you. Remember that being too loud can also make you come across as rude and unpleasant, so always keep the balance.

Practice all of this on a regular basis, and it will soon become second nature to you. It is important to look warm, friendly, and confident, but do not overthink this issue. Many people end up pretending to be something that they really aren't in the process of trying to appear impressive and attractive. Be authentic, feel comfortable, and do your best. It is however important that you reflect on your performance after every event, at least during the early days of your networking journey. This will help you to feel more confident and make the necessary changes to improve yourself on the basis of not just your own judgment but also the reactions of other people.

4. WORK ON IMPROVING YOUR INTERPERSONAL SKILLS

These aren't the same as the regular communication skills we discussed above. Interpersonal skills are about understanding the other person, taking cues from their body language, and making sense of the conversation the right way. Say, for example, that you are at an event and you see somebody smiling at you. This clearly shows that they are interested in a conversation, but they might be too shy to take the first step. People sometimes make the mistake of taking this as being dismissed and end up missing an opportunity to socialize. Observing people and trying to understand them through their body language as well as their speech is very important. Some things cannot be said and will never be said, they have to be understood. If you notice this person who smiled at you, you will easily be able to figure out that they are just shy.

Understanding people is part observation and part practice. When someone you meet feels that you understand them, it will really put them at ease and help you both have a beautiful and useful relationship with one another. Doing this well also makes getting along with different personality types much easier.

5. LEARN TO USE THE MAGIC OF HUMOR

Putting a smile on someone's face is the best way to build a bond with them. Humor helps to lighten the mood and can help ease even the tensest personality or situation. It can present you as a fun person to talk to and help build trust. This quality isn't just a mood lifter for others. It also enables you to look and feel good and positive. If you are naturally blessed with a good sense of humor, using it at networking events wouldn't be very difficult. Manage your jitters, feel comfortable and you will easily be able to get laughs echoing all around you.

If cracking jokes and hilarious one-liners is not your forte, worry not because this skill is not impossible to learn. Feeling comfortable and being able to be yourself is key if you want to add humor to your repertoire of skills. Comedy shows on television and YouTube are a good place to start. Try to observe what these people say and how they say it. You might have already noticed that a person who has a reputation for being funny doesn't have to do much to get laughs. Creating that image for yourself will take time, practice, and patience. Take it slow and be sure not to offend anyone in the process. The safest place to start is to make jokes about yourself. Humor, when done the right way, can weave magic, but if it goes wrong, it can also turn into a disaster for you. Working on this skill can be greatly beneficial to you in your social relationships. Laughter generates the release of serotonin, which is the happy hormone in your body, and this can help uplift your spirits and spread positivity and light all around you. Who on earth wouldn't like to socialize with such a person?

6. BE RESPECTFUL

This is the most basic and fundamental networking skill you must possess. Whether it's through your words or actions, disrespecting someone is the last thing you want to do at a social event. On several occasions, we don't intend to be disrespectful but some of our behaviors come across as rude. There could be many reasons behind this, including your cultural background, your upbringing, the habits you picked up over the years, the kind of people you are surrounded by most of the time or just differences in personality types. Work to find out if any aspect of your behavior reflects a lack of respect. Speaking over another person is a habit for some people, but this might seem rude to the individual on the receiving end. Imagine, for example, that you are in a conversation with a person who is in a rush to put forth their views and doesn't allow you the space to express your opinion or point. Wouldn't you feel annoyed? Wouldn't such behavior make you feel that you are not being heard? It would be because it's disrespectful. Another behavior you must rid yourself of or avoid is related to listening properly. You know how important it is to listen attentively when you are in a conversation with someone, and what happens when you don't? "Sorry? Can you please say that again? Sorry I didn't get you," and other phrases like these come up. It is normal and absolutely okay to use them occasionally, but repeating them over and over again during a meeting will make your connection feel that you are not paying attention to them and are ignoring them. Respectful and polite people always thrive at networking events because they are approachable, understanding, and nice to interact with. That's who you want to be.

If you happen to travel abroad for a networking event or are about to meet someone from a different culture or nationality and are not sure about what would be the right social etiquette and what would be deemed respectful, it's always a good idea to do some research prior to the event. The internet is full of information, and you will in most cases be surely able to find details about good social and behavioral rules in most countries of the world. If you don't have the time to do all of that, it never hurts to ask, and if something goes wrong or you end up making a mistake, a polite apology can in most cases do the job for you. To err is human, and owning up to it is a sign of a mature and well-developed mind and a strong and confident personality.

7. EXUDE CONFIDENCE

This can most definitely be called the strongest and the most powerful weapon for anyone wanting to build their social capital. Confidence is about how you say what you say, and the surety with which you speak. It shows up in every aspect of your personality, from the way you walk into a room to the way you say goodbye. A confident person always stands out in a crowd and is hard to miss. While some people are naturally confident, others are not. Here are some things you can do to improve on this vital trait:

- Always keep eye contact with the speaker.

- Prepare a few go-to topics to talk about just in case you run out of words at that moment. This will help to tackle the nervousness that comes with awkward silences in a conversation.

- Use positive affirmations every morning to reprogram your subconscious mind and fill your system with confidence. Look at yourself in the mirror and say lines like, "I am super confident, I can handle every social interaction and networking event with ease, I am awesome and I feel great today." This is a scientifically proven method that, if used over time, can really help you become a confident personality. Repeat it to yourself every time you feel low about yourself, and you will soon start feeling better.

- Fake it till you make it. Look at the body language of any person who you feel is confident, and just copy it mechanically. As you do it over and over again, your mind will be tricked to believe that you are really feeling confident and will start aligning itself with your body language by secreting hormones that actually make a person feel good and positive.

- Wear something that makes you feel beautiful from the inside out. Do you have a favorite dress? Is there a piece of jewelry that particularly uplifts you? Put that on when you have a networking event to attend, and it will serve as a natural and instant confidence booster for you.

- Think back to a moment in your past when you felt particularly confident. We all have such times when we look in the mirror and feel good about ourselves. Try to channel those emotions into your present moment. How was your mindset then? What was your thought process like? Try to replicate it, and if you cannot, at least just pretend like you are in the same situation right now. If anything, this trick will help to keep your confidence level high throughout the event at which you want to present yourself well.

- Be positive at all times. Undesirable and unfavorable experiences of life often create negativity in our minds, and this slowly translates into a pessimistic thought process. We begin doubting ourselves and this consequently depletes our self-confidence. Make a conscious attempt to stay away from negative self-talk. Every time an unwanted thought crosses your mind, actively push it away and follow it up with good thoughts to dilute its negative impact. Don't let negative people and circumstances crush your self-confidence and ruin your life. The journey of entrepreneurship and the associated task of growing your social capital are not easy for anyone, and you are not alone in it. Millions have done it before you, and millions more will do it after you as well. So, work to inculcate positive thinking, and self-confidence will automatically follow. Further to this, positivity can also help you face unfavorable outcomes, i.e., when things don't go your way or when your prospects do not respond the way you want them to.

Nobody is super confident at all times. Everyone has their low phases, even those who seem like the most self-assured people around you. So you don't have to feel ashamed if you aren't all that confident. Embrace who you are, and work to improve.

8. PRACTICE YOUR PUBLIC SPEAKING SKILLS

Communication is an essential element of networking, and public speaking is an important facet of communication. When you network, you might opt to take up leadership roles in the social organization you are part of. You might be in charge of the task of handling a certain event or be appointed to run the show as the chairman or secretary. Whatever the role, giving speeches and generally speaking in public would be an integral part of your job. It is, therefore, important that you work on polishing your public speaking skills and learn to tackle social anxiety and nervousness. A pounding heart and trembling hands are absolutely normal physiological reactions that almost all people experience when placed in a public setting. Don't associate this with anything negative. The adrenaline rush in your system might cause you to sweat, but this doesn't mean that you will perform poorly or make a fool of yourself. The best way to manage the fear of speaking in public is to prepare, prepare, and then prepare some more. Go over your notes several times, practice your speech, videotape yourself, get a friend to critique your performance, and do whatever it takes for you to feel comfortable and at ease with what you have to say. Let your personality shine through and just be your natural self. Try not to read as much as possible and work from an outline instead. Nobody would be interested in listening to a robotic delivery of words. You don't need to strive to be totally perfect, all you have to do is capture the interest of your audience. Use your hands, try to eliminate nervous gestures, add a bit of humor, and include a story in your speech to give it a personal touch. If you succeed at getting a good initial response from your listeners, you will automatically begin to feel confident and your system will pump up your energy to help you deliver the rest of your talk well too. In order to achieve this, always make it a point to start on an interesting note. Instead of saying, "Today I am going to talk to you about…," start with a shocking statistic or a fascinating anecdote. In the end, finish with a strong statement to leave the audience amazed. The reaction of your audience is in essence a measure of your success at public speaking.

9. GET THERE EARLY

Making a last-minute protagonist entry might work for parties, but when you're attending a networking event, you should always try to be there early. Leave ample time for you to find the venue, park your car, and get to the exact location of the event. You don't want to be hunting around for the address or struggling to find a parking space for your car in the parking lot with the clock ticking. Networking events can be daunting, especially if you are going alone, and joining in late will only add to the anxiety. Do you fear that scenario in which you are stuck with your business cards and a drink in one corner of the room while the others are happily chatting away in a large group on the other side? If yes, then you should be an early bird. Jumping in before time will keep you away from getting lost in the crowd or feeling out of place. You will be able to meet people in small bunches and at a much more relaxed pace, and this will help you stay in the thick of things throughout the event. Your target should therefore be to reach the location while the group is small.

Another great advantage of arriving early is that you will have the time to bond with the organizers of the event. They are the ones who brought in all the people you would be networking with, so you should go ahead and introduce yourself at the least. Being on time would also mean you have a larger window to network when compared to those arriving late. Those quiet moments at the start can also help you to tackle your nerves and settle in before the party actually begins. As part of your preparation before the event, you should scan the guest list to get a brief overview of who's attending and use social media to familiarize yourself with the faces. Some extra time at the event will then come in handy for you to recollect the faces, organize your thoughts and approach the people you're most keen on connecting with.

Bobbing in and out of networking events isn't for everyone. If you are an introvert and hate being around people, this might seem particularly hard. Many self-described introverts feel that the networking world isn't for them. Dazzling people with their confidence and charm feels like an impossible task to them. So does this mean that networking is only for outgoing, extroverted personalities? Are all of the amazing benefits of building social capital supposed to be inaccessible to introverts? No. Introverts can network too and can do it amazingly well. Here are some tips to help you with it if you're an introvert.

- Embrace your personality and work around it. The major difference between introverts and extroverts is in the way they recharge and build up their energy levels. While extroverts feel energized when they are among people, introverts require some quiet time to rejuvenate and recover. So if you think you fall in the latter category, plan some relaxing activities for yourself before and after every networking event. It could be a relaxing bath, time at the spa, a quiet walk outside, reading a book, or any other solo activity that has a proven track record of relaxing your body and mind. This time cushion around the event will prepare you and pump you up, putting you on par with your extroverted counterparts.

- Tailor your expectations to your personality type. What is comfortable for someone else might not be so for you, and vice versa. Instead of aiming to meet a large number of people and collecting about 25 to 30 business cards in one event, target a smaller number and focus on making two or three meaningful connections instead. Play to your strengths rather than following the norm. There is a ubiquitous presumption out there that introverts aren't good at interacting with people. This, however, is just a myth. The only thing they cannot do is interact in the same way extroverts do, and there is nothing wrong with that. Since two people cannot ever be entirely the same, how can their ways of socializing be?

- Find a way to solve the introduction problem. Entering a room full of strangers and introducing yourself might be very nerve-wracking for you if you are an introverted personality. This shouldn't prevent you from socializing. Try to arrive at the event early and get in touch with one of the organizers. Share your goal and purpose behind attending the event with them, and get their advice/suggestions on who you should meet. Be very specific when describing your purpose so that you are matched with the right people. Be sure to highlight those aspects about you that are unique and likely to add value to the lives of other people. Once you have a few names, politely request the organizer to introduce you to them when they arrive. Meeting a new person alongside somebody else as opposed to doing it all alone will be so much easier. You won't have to worry about freezing up in the company of someone unknown to you, and the entire event will be a smooth and productive ride for you. Having someone with you at the start of an interaction doesn't mean that you won't have to talk at all. In order to ensure that you have the right words to speak when the situation demands, have a set of unusual questions and icebreakers prepared beforehand and use them when needed.

- Listen more and talk less. You absolutely need no practice or preparation to do this. It will come naturally to you due to your introversion. Speaking less, which you would have always categorized as your weakness, can now be used as your strength. The importance of being an active listener has already been emphasized enough earlier in the chapter. It is a great way to make others feel valued. Speak a few lines here and there throughout the conversation, but largely focus on listening attentively to what the opposite person has to say. Refrain from looking at your phone or observing other people in the room. Show interest and be patient. Ask interesting and unique questions to keep the conversation flowing. Adopting this strategy of listening more will take away most of your nervousness and will put you at ease. You will be surprised to see how effective a technique this can be to help you succeed at building your social capital.

- Set a time limit for every networking event you attend. Awkwardness and discomfort can on many occasions tempt you to leave early, but make it a point to spend a minimum of 30 to 40 minutes there. When stuck in a corner with nobody to talk to, most people make the mistake of picking up their phone to appear important, even if what they're doing is scrolling through their social media feed. Constantly looking at your phone in the midst of a conversation is a sign of disinterest and disrespect, and doing so when you are alone can make people feel that you are not interested in a conversation. The awkwardness you are trying to beat by keeping yourself busy in the virtual world will only increase if you stay focused on your mobile phone. Put your phone away for the duration of the meeting, keeping it in a place you cannot easily access. Make an attempt to start a conversation with at least one person, and even if that fails or doesn't continue for long, push yourself to do it one more time with someone new.

Always remember that you are an entrepreneur, and perseverance is in your blood. As you keep doing this and getting engrossed, you won't even realize when the 30 minutes will pass and you might even end up staying for longer than you initially planned to.

- Don't let uncomfortable situations and awkward moments deter you from socializing. No matter how much you prepare yourself, it would be unrealistic to expect every interaction to be positive and comfortable. If you find someone to be too negative or unpleasant to speak to, you can always politely excuse yourself from the conversation. Relationships are meant to be formed with those you feel some kind of a positive connection. Human interactions can be messy, and giving yourself a breather can help you get yourself back in the right mindset for the event. Your personality type can also pose challenges for you. You might suddenly run out of the right words in the middle of a sentence, end up making a false or unpleasant start, or just fumble with something out of fear. Don't allow yourself to feel ashamed or embarrassed in circumstances like these. Take a deep breath, smile and get on with the next activity. The more attention you give to mistakes like these, the more they will consume you and spoil your day. Stay focused on your ultimate goal of achieving a wealth of social connections, and don't let little stumbling blocks like these hamper your progress.

- Learn to manage your inner critic. When you end up at an event that is not the best fit for your personality type, your inner voice can start weaving negative thoughts. "I am boring, I am not worth it, nobody would want to talk to me," are some statements that might start building up in your mind. As soon as you begin to feel this way, work to eliminate these thoughts and start thinking something positive about yourself. These pessimistic thoughts, if not managed, will give rise to negative emotions and end up lowering your confidence and energy levels. This is the last thing you want for yourself when you are about to attend a networking event. Do whatever it takes to keep your energy levels high. Have a healthy meal so that you are well-fuelled up for the hours ahead. Avoid overprocessed junk food. Try listening to some music on the way to the event to keep your mind occupied. Wearing a scent you like or a fragrance that is known to have soothing and calming properties can also be greatly beneficial. Having this scent in your car whilst you are on a commute, or a sachet of it in your pocket would be a good idea. It is better you avoid consuming caffeine because this will only add to your anxiety. In case you would like to have a beverage, try something cold to help numb your system and feel cool from within. Some people feel that consuming a bit of alcohol can give them the necessary boost of energy and positivity, but this is not a good idea and can instead make you appear unprofessional. Every fear and every negative thought is only in your mind. Learn to manage it, and half your job is done.

Introverts can be mighty successful at networking. They have within them the strengths and skills to socialize effectively. All that is needed is to be able to bring them out in the right way. We all have preferences, likes, dislikes, and priorities around which we build our lives. Whether you are an introvert or an extrovert, working to maximize your strengths and down-play your weaknesses is what will bring you ultimate success at networking. Take the time to understand yourself and tailor your networking approach accordingly. What are those aspects of socializing that make you uncomfortable? What are you particularly anxious about? What makes you nervous? What do you most enjoy about social events? It is not important to follow the herd. True sensibility lies in identifying the techniques that work for you. Finally, it is important that you learn to love networking. Despite all your challenges, try to change your mindset and look at networking as an opportunity rather than a chore. In the world we live in, social capital is almost a necessity. Whether we like it or hate it, we have to invest our time in building it for the myriad of benefits it can provide. When there is a networking event you are obliged to attend, you can look at it in two ways. You can tell yourself, "I hate it and I will have to now put on a show." On the other hand, you could also say, "This might be interesting." When you season what you already dislike with negative self-talk, it will only make your experience all the more difficult and boring.

Changing your mindset and inculcating one that looks at networking in a favorable light is not difficult. When you like what you do, the results are always better. So, make the effort to love the process of building your social capital, and this activity will seem so much more easy and fun.

The final stage of a social relationship is one in which the trust between two parties leads to the creation of an alliance. In the next chapter, we will explore the subject of business alliances and provide you with all the knowledge you will need to take your social relationships to the next level.

CHAPTER SEVEN:

·····························

ALL ABOUT BUSINESS ALLIANCES

What happens when two things come together? Something bigger and better than what the individual parts can independently accomplish is created, and if the combination is right, the resulting product can be truly magical. When we set foot into the arena of networking, this is the kind of great outcome we all expect. Following the steps, tips, and tricks discussed so far will give you a good start in this direction, and an understanding of the contents of this chapter can help you take your networking efforts to the next level. So what is the next level in the context of networking? It's a business alliance. Also called a strategic alliance, a business alliance is an arrangement between two companies. This alliance is created for the mutual benefit of the parties involved. The contract on which such a relationship is based can be as simple or complicated as you want it to be. It doesn't have to always be as detailed as a joint venture agreement, or necessarily involve the pooling of resources or the establishment of a separate legal entity. In a business alliance, two businesses agree to work towards a common goal whilst keeping their independence intact.

The relationship thus created doesn't have to be a permanent one. It could be short- or long-term, and the agreement could be formal or informal. The alliance might also be focused on a particular set of customers, a few products or services, or businesses in a certain region. Business alliances are usually created when companies want to enter a new market, expand their product line, develop an edge over a competitor or create a more effective process of getting a job done. This kind of arrangement can help a company achieve organic growth in a much faster and more efficient way. It is a powerful way for companies to collaborate, share resources, and reduce costs. No business in the world can excel at everything. You, as the owner of an enterprise, will need to collaborate with other businesses and leverage each other's resources to solve problems and attain success. This is where the need for business alliances arises.

One popular real-world example of a business alliance is the agreement between Starbucks and Barnes & Noble. While the former brews the coffee, the latter provides a venue where coffee can be enjoyed. Both companies are doing what they do best whilst sharing the cost of space. The co-branded B&N cafés help both companies to capture new markets and retain existing customers. Another well-known example is the strategic alliance between Starbucks and Target. Walk into any of the thousands of Target stores out there, and you will find a Starbucks counter waiting to refresh you. This partnership was formed in 1999 and has been going strong ever since.

Any business, irrespective of its size and industry, can form a strategic alliance with another company that has the potential to improve its position and bottom line. A pharmaceutical company can form an agreement with a research laboratory to invent new drugs, a fashion retailer can strike a deal with a contract manufacturer to ensure the production of high-quality apparel, and an online publication such as a magazine or newspaper business can form an alliance with a social media analytics and marketing company to improve its promotional strategies and outcomes. By sharing resources such as raw materials, office space, and manufacturing facilities, companies can lower their cost of production, thereby enjoying greater sales volumes and a higher profit margin. Joined purchasing agreements and shared distribution networks are among the many methods companies use to minimize costs for both parties. When two companies form an alliance, they end up sharing their strengths to downplay the weaknesses of the parties involved. For instance, company A might have a strong sales force but may lack engineering talent, and company B might be exceptional with regard to their engineering talent but have a poorly performing sales team. An alliance between company A and company B can help both of them overcome their weaknesses providing them with greater market reach and growth opportunities. All in all, getting into a business alliance can be really advantageous for your entrepreneurial venture. It can take you to places you cannot go alone and can help you accomplish what is unimaginable for a business to get to all by itself. The concept of forming an alliance with another business whose products or services go well with yours is not just alluring but is also critical for you to be able to stay competitive in the market.

As good as the consequences of establishing a business alliance seem, getting to that pinnacle of success with your social connections isn't a cakewalk. You need to know when the right time to begin thinking about an alliance is. You met someone at an industry event and felt good about the person and the interaction you had with them. So, you may think, let's partner with this person on a project. But this would be a premature move. Rushing things to see results or derive an advantage from a connection will take you nowhere in your networking journey. You need to first get to know each other well by meeting a few more times, and invest the time and effort to deepen and strengthen your bond before diving into something as big as an alliance. Business alliances are not simple. They can be very tricky if not handled correctly. An alliance will only work as long as it is beneficial for both parties involved. So what is it that you as an entrepreneur can do to ensure your alliance is successful? Here are a few tips and pointers to keep in mind.

1. IDENTIFY THE NEED

The most important thing that will keep an alliance afloat is its objective. Finding a strong connection from your social network to form an alliance with is not the end of the story. While it is important that you develop a good amount of trust with a person before getting into any sort of partnership with them, determining why you want to do so is equally crucial. In what ways do you think you and the other company will benefit if you both decide to come together? What are your aims, objectives, mission, and vision for your business, and where does this company you wish to make an alliance with fit in to help you achieve them? Take a close look at your strengths and weaknesses, and try to do the same for the other party as well. Do you have a resource that the other is lacking? Will forming a partnership increase both your production capacities? In what way do you and the other company complement one another? The more time you put into this kind of analysis at the start, the easier and more fruitful your journey ahead will be.

We all know BMW and Louis Vuitton. Both of these brands belong to very different industries, but they're also quite similar in many ways. The most important commonality is that both Louis Vuitton and BMW are luxury brands. This simply means that those who can afford a BMW car can most likely also afford to buy a Louis Vuitton handbag. So what does this imply? Both brands have a shared audience/customer base. This was probably the reason why the two companies formed an alliance with one another. The partnership involved the creation of themed handbags to match the design of the BMW I8 sports car. The specially launched collection comprised a four-piece bag set made using carbon fiber. This material is rarely used in handbags but was chosen to go with the carbon fiber used in the inner cell of the car. The sleek black outer color and electric blue lining of the bag also matched the car's design perfectly. An alliance of this kind could help both brands increase their sales volume for the particular products and also widen their customer base. Imagine Louis Vuitton forming an alliance with Ford. This alliance would surely not have worked as well as the BMW-Louis Vuitton partnership. These custom-made handbags retailed at a whopping $20,000, but this price is surely not unreasonable for someone willing to spend more than $130,000 on a car. Compare this with a customer who likes to buy a Ford for around $40,000. You can easily predict what the outcome of a Louis Vuitton-Ford alliance for a similar product will be. No matter how strong the relationship between the owners of Ford and Louis Vuitton is, an alliance of this kind will simply not work. It is, therefore, important that you have a clear understanding of what you will bring to the table and what the other company will do, what you expect from the deal, and what you want to gain from it.

2. EVALUATE THE PARTNER

Once you have completed the first step of determining the need for an alliance, your next course of action should be to research the firm you wish to partner with. No matter who introduced you to this contact, be it a close friend or a trusted business associate, carrying out thorough research about them before getting into any sort of contractual relationship is important. You might be wondering, "I trust this person, and I know that an alliance between us could bring a promising future for both, then what should I research?" Forming a business alliance with someone means that you will have to work with them. It is therefore essential for you to know about their management style and see if that suits you. What are the work ethics and values of your potential partner? Do you feel comfortable with their work style? Clashes are inevitable in a relationship, so what are those areas in which you could possibly clash? You do not want to find yourself in a relationship in which the other party is your polar opposite. Here are a few questions you must find answers to through your research.

- How is work done at the other company?

- Is the work environment fast-paced or laid-back?

- Who will be in charge of payments?

- How and by when can you expect to be
  paid for your part of the work?

- Who is in charge of managing client relationships?

- How are decisions made?

Try to find out as much as you can about the company. Getting inside information from employees is a good idea if you have access to them. You could also try asking the person who referred you to this business for useful information about the management of the enterprise. The same person can also put you in touch with people working in the company to help you get a different perspective about its work environment. Many entrepreneurs make the mistake of relying solely on online research for this kind of information.

While reviews from employees on job portals and other professional websites could provide you with a rough idea about the functioning of the firm, it would be unrealistic to hope for a clear and undistorted image. Employees also often do not provide a clear picture due to the fear of legal retribution, so relying on references wouldn't work. Use a combination of all of these techniques along with the information you managed to gather through your personal interactions with the owner/management of the business and carry out a comparative study of both companies. Are they similar or different? If they are similar, how similar? If they are different, is it still possible to find a way to minimize these differences and form an alliance?

3. ESTABLISH JOINT OBJECTIVES & GOALS

You might have reasons for getting into an alliance with your potential partner and they might have them too, but an alliance is not about individual goals. Both you and your potential partner must work to establish joint objectives for this combined chapter of your careers. Keep your expectations real. The goals and objectives you lay down must reflect what both parties aspire to and expect to gain from this arrangement. Nobody would want to be a part of an alliance in which one party is giving almost everything to the relationship and the other is enjoying a free ride. It won't take long for such a partnership to turn sour and crash. The goals must be created in accordance with the resources both parties are bringing in. Every entity that is a part of the alliance must benefit from it. If one feels that they are not gaining as much as the other or in line with their expectations or projections, the alliance will not last long and conflicts will occur. Take, for example, the Starbucks-Target partnership we discussed above. By placing the Starbucks counter inside the Target store itself, the companies involved have tried to ensure that both are in the line of view of customers. More and more people will want to visit Target because of the delicious Starbucks beverages and snacks available at the store to fuel their shopping trip. On the other end, Starbucks lovers will choose this counter to enjoy a coffee or have a bite because they get to shop at the same place. Now, assume for a moment that Starbucks didn't have a counter there, and there was only a tiny kitchen located in some dark corner with no branding to identify it. The shoppers at Target would still have the opportunity to enjoy some refreshments after spending hours at the store strolling down aisles, but no one would know that it's Starbucks giving them the pleasure. Do you think Starbucks would ever agree to get into such a partnership even if Target agrees to pay them a high amount of money for it? It is important to think fairly from the sides of both parties when you set out to create the objectives for your alliance. Always remember the golden rule of networking we discussed earlier. Think and act in the best interest of the other party, and success will automatically come your way.

4. DEFINE RULES & RESPONSIBILITIES

Working with a new bunch of people you aren't familiar with is not easy. There is a world of difference between socializing with someone occasionally at networking events and interacting with them at the workplace on a day-to-day basis. The quickest way to make this journey easy for both parties is to define the rules and responsibilities of the game. Who does what, and who is in charge of which aspect? When you form an alliance with another company, both of you will bring in resources to make things work. It is natural that you will require people to manage these resources and carry out the operations of the alliance. Decide beforehand how many people each company will bring in to fulfill the job. Many alliances fail because of poor management. A lot of problems can be avoided if there are well-defined rules in place to govern every aspect of business and if every member is clear about what each one is required to do. Let's revisit the Starbucks-Barnes & Noble alliance once again. The B&N cafés are a joint initiative involving labor and capital contribution from both parties, and there are thousands of such cafés around the world. The idea behind this is that people could enjoy a cup of coffee and a book at the same time. In order to ensure that these outlets run successfully, someone will need to keep stock of the books, the ingredients for the coffee and snacks, the quality of service, the cleanliness and hygiene at the place, the overall atmosphere and environment at the cafe, and much more. This means that qualified professionals will be required to manage these outlets both on the ground and on the back end. To ensure that these people coming from different organizations work as a unified whole and give their best, they will need to be comfortable and clear with their roles. Dividing the work, delegating responsibilities, and setting boundaries will also help to make sure that operations flow smoothly at all cafés every day. The broader objective of any alliance is to leverage the strengths of both parties, and this can be best achieved only when the basic affairs of operations and management are well taken care of.

5. ESTABLISH A CLEAR COMMUNICATION PROCESS

Good communication between members is key if you wish to create an enduring alliance. This simple skill has the power to make or break a business. When you are working with someone, there is a lot you will need to talk about on a daily and weekly basis. Those working on the ground will need to be clear about their line of communication. Not just that, but those at the management level will also need to exchange sales reports and performance details, and also discuss strategies to grow the alliance. You, as an entrepreneur, will need to have meetings with the owner of the other company to analyze and evaluate your progress periodically. Effective communication is essential at every level. It is, therefore, important that when you form the alliance, you must clearly discuss and document the communication pattern you wish to follow. Here are some questions you should try to answer:

- Who will be the primary contact person from both companies?

- Who will be in charge of reporting periodic performance data to the management on both sides?

- How often will management meetings be held?

You must work to develop your relationship in such a way that both parties are able to communicate their suggestions and recommendations to one another without any hesitation. Disappointments and misunderstandings can be avoided a great deal if systematic work processes are established to carry out business. Your style and views with regard to communication might be different from that of your partner. So having a candid discussion about the same early on in your journey together could help set things right. Whether it is running your business alliance, resolving a conflict, evaluating your performance, or anything else, nothing can be accomplished without communication. You should therefore never make the mistake of ignoring this crucial element.

6. DEVELOP CONFLICT RESOLUTION SYSTEMS

No alliance in the world is a match made in heaven or a bed of roses. There will be good times, but there will be bad ones too. Where there are people, there will be differences in opinions, ideas, and capabilities, and all of this can result in conflict among the people working for you and with you. The best thing you can do is to be prepared for it and have a plan to tackle the worst. What course of action will you take if and when a conflict arises? How will you communicate your point to the other party? How will you deal with an unresponsive partner? What will be your reaction when your partner disagrees with you? Your approach will most likely be closely tied to the kind of person you are. If this is your first time working in partnership with another entrepreneur, take the time to understand yourself and visualize the scenarios you might face. If you are a short-tempered person, set aside some strategies you will use to remain calm during those moments. You don't want your arrangement to fall apart due to a petty argument or ego clash. No two people can ever be the same, and you should remind yourself of this to yourself as often as you can. Always keep your eye on the bigger picture, and focus on resolving the issue rather than blaming one another. Always act sensibly, compromise when necessary, and do everything you can to keep things together. If you, however, land in a situation in which keeping the alliance going is next to impossible, finish the relationship amicably before you go your separate ways. It always helps to be prepared for the breakup of the alliance, so have an exit plan worked out well in advance. Anything is easier to handle if you have a pre-written action plan to guide you.

One point that you must always keep in mind is that you are more than the entrepreneur in you. Your business is an important part of your life, but there is definitely more to your personality than just that. So, if you were unsuccessful in establishing an alliance with another entrepreneur, it doesn't mean you have to break all ties with them. Your business alliance didn't work, but you can still be buddies. You can hang out with one another at social events, be each other's cheerleaders by providing referrals, and help each other build your social capital. If you end your alliance on a positive note, your partner will carry a positive image of you everywhere they go and this will only benefit you. A happy ending also makes it so much easier to work with the same person in a different capacity in the future or to form an alliance with another successful entrepreneur who is known to them. People aren't bad, circumstances are. So, do not let one sour relationship close many other doors of opportunities for you in your career.

7. BE PATIENT

Business alliances take time to work and generate results. You cannot expect your efforts to bear fruit overnight. Your job and the people involved in it may not seem all that comfortable at the start, but be patient and keep trying. You are as new to them as they are to you, so allow them the time to settle in. Like in any new activity, there may be mistakes and even blunders during the early days of your venture. Do not judge anyone at this stage, and avoid the temptation of jumping to conclusions. Try to learn from every experience instead of complaining, and take things slowly. If your idea has been thoroughly analyzed and evaluated before implementation, have confidence in your work and keep putting in the effort to create the success story you had dreamt of. Try to find ways to stand out.

8. DEMONSTRATE COMMITMENT

Every project, whether small or large, is important in its own way. The alliance you form should also be given the status it deserves. Both parties must be willing to invest the time and effort to grow it. Your actions must demonstrate that you are fully committed to this project, and this holds true for your partner as well. The main objective of any alliance is to make an impact. If the people at the top aren't willing to nurture and care for it, the purpose is lost and the partnership has no meaning. You must actively engage yourself in the workings of the project and must not hesitate to even break contractual boundaries and obligations to make it work. Committed partners face risks, put in all the effort needed, and do everything that's in their power to ensure the alliance sees the light of day and success. It is important that you are committed and the partner you wish to work with is as well. Without an adequate amount of passion and hard work, even the most brilliant project ideas will not succeed.

9. FORMALIZE THE ALLIANCE

A formal agreement is a founding document on which most organizations and projects are based. It defines the relationship in great detail and serves as proof of the alliance for both parties. Having a formal agreement isn't mandatory for anyone forming a strategic alliance, but drafting one is never a bad idea. It can protect you during times when goals, expectations, and activities are not in line with what had been outlined. In case a dispute arises between both parties regarding what was agreed or on any other matter concerning the functioning, rights, and responsibilities of partners, you will have a document to refer back to in order to solve the conflict. The kind of agreement you will need to create will depend upon the type of alliance you are getting into.

There are three kinds of business alliances commonly used by corporate leaders around the world today. The first is called a joint venture. This is quite a popular form of partnership that involves the creation of a new entity. For example, companies X and C will join to create a child company known as company Z. It is quite similar to a normal company, except that it has two owners. Both parties work together to accomplish a common goal and share the profits of the enterprise in an agreed ratio. Here are some real-life examples of popular companies that entered into a joint venture with another giant to create something bigger and better. Google's parent company, Alphabet, formed a joint venture with pharmaceuticals megacorp Glaxo and Smith to produce bio-electric medicines. The ratio of ownership was 45% to 55%, and the venture began operations in 2016. The entity thus created is called "Galvani Bioelectronics," and the goal is to carry out research on the idea of treating diseases using electrical signals. The taxi company Uber and the heavy vehicles manufacturer Volvo also came together to produce driverless cars in a 50:50 joint venture. Microsoft and General Electric and Sony and Ericsson are other well-known examples of this kind of business alliance. If one company owns a greater share in the business than the other (for example, if company A owns 70% and company B has a 30% holding) such a joint venture is called a majority-owned venture.

The second kind of strategic alliance you can consider forming is an equity strategic alliance. As the name suggests, this type of partnership involves the purchase of equities. This is done in one of two ways. The first method is known as partial acquisition in which one company purchases equities from the other. The second way is one in which both companies purchase equities in each other's businesses, and is called a cross-equity transaction. One popular example of an equity strategic alliance is the Tesla and Panasonic partnership. It began with an investment of $30 million by Panasonic in Tesla to improve battery technology for electric vehicles. The alliance grew further, and the two companies established a lithium-ion battery plant in Nevada, United States.

The third and final type of strategic alliance is a non-equity alliance. This could be called the simplest form of business alliance because it doesn't involve the creation of a business entity or the purchase of equities. It is quite informal and loose when compared to a joint venture or an equity alliance. Due to this reason, this alliance type is the most popular in the business world. Pick out the data on strategic alliances around the world, and the non-equity one will take the top spot. One popular example of a non-equity strategic alliance is the Starbucks Kroger partnership. Kroger is the most popular grocery store in the United States, and this partnership enables its customers to enjoy Starbucks beverages and snacks right inside their shopping haven. If you look at this partnership closely, you will find that these two companies haven't created any new organizations. Neither of them holds any ownership rights in each other's businesses either, and the two are totally independent as entities. The only link between the two companies that allows

Kroger to sell Starbucks in their store is the license. Kroger has permission from Starbucks to use its brand name for the benefit of both parties, and this is what their business alliance is all about.

The type of alliance you choose to adopt will depend upon several factors. What is your objective behind this partnership, and how long do you think it will take to accomplish it? How much time do you have on hand to complete the starting up formalities, and how much effort are you willing to put in? What is the level of trust between you and your partner? What is the nature of your business? Is it high-risk, highly competitive, or rather stable? Think critically about all these aspects before you make the final choice for the type of organization you want. Any business alliance can be successful if:

- It mitigates a significant risk for the business or the parties.

- The purpose for which it forms is critical for the parties to achieve the overall objective of their primary business. For example, if company A, an American automobile manufacturer, gets into an alliance with company B, a French fashion retailer, to capture the French market, then gaining market share in France should be a part of the primary objective of the company.

- It blocks a competitive threat for the parties involved.

- It creates strategic options/choices for the companies in the alliance.

- Both parties have a strong trusting relationship and work consistently to maintain/improve it.

Every activity in business comes with a risk and a reward, and this is true for strategic alliances as well. Despite all the benefits they can bring to your business, strategic alliances aren't without their challenges. Working with different people can be difficult. Managing the newly formed entity might not be easy because of institutional differences. Since both companies share confidential information with one another, there is a high risk of data misuse. There are hidden costs associated with the alliance which may show themselves up later on and impact the profitability of the venture. The company which has an upper hand in the alliance may misuse its position and deviate from the planned objectives. These might be tricky situations for the parties involved in an alliance, but with the right amount of care and caution, all of these can be avoided or managed quite well. As Gide said, "You cannot discover new oceans unless you have the courage to lose sight of the shore." Networking and the social capital you build are oceans of endless possibilities, and a business alliance is a treasure you could find if you persist and toil enough. So, nurture your social relationships, invest in them, work for them, and give them your everything with sincerity and you will be surprised to see all of it come back to you with a gilded touch and in larger amounts than you expended.

CHAPTER EIGHT:

....

THE NETWORKING NO-NOS

In the 1960s, when the world was just beginning to feel the impact of computers, something extraordinary was taking place in the Lakeside school located in the Seattle area of Washington. Among the many boys and girls that attended the school was one boy who liked to spend more time in the computer center than in the classroom. He was rarely allowed inside, but he still wanted to be there. He had a deep passion for programming and could be seen hovering around the smart machines with a desire to learn about them. He peeped through doors and windows to listen to the programmers working inside and to make sense of what they were up to. The trash can in the computer center was one thing he had easy and unrestricted access to, and this eventually became his treasure trove of knowledge. After the programmers left, this boy would dig through the bin and remove the torn pieces of paper. He would then put these pieces together to read the text printed on them. All of what he was reading were programming errors. He did this every day and soon had a collection of the mistakes one could make when writing code and working with computer programs. Learning what won't work made him a programming genius, and this boy was the man we know today as the billionaire business tycoon and founder of Microsoft, William Henry Gates III, or simply Bill Gates.

Knowing how to get something right can bring you success, but having an understanding of the ways in which you could possibly go wrong can as well. In this chapter, we will discuss what you shouldn't do as you go about building your social capital.

1. DON'T USE EMAIL AS YOUR MAIN METHOD OF NETWORKING

Email has revolutionized the way we communicate today. We use it for everything, both professionally as well as personally. This invention could however turn into a curse if you do not use it the right way. Many entrepreneurs make the mistake of using emails to introduce themselves to a new social contact and also to build and maintain that relationship. Emails are a quick and easy way to send a note to someone, but this could work to your disadvantage if your recipient doesn't interpret it correctly. As discussed earlier, you must try your best to have a live interaction with your connections. If a face-to-face meeting isn't possible, opt for a video or phone conversation instead of relying entirely on emails. Your contacts won't be able to establish a facial connection with you via email, and making sense of plain text without any emotions, voice, or gestures to support it could result in misunderstandings and a rather shallow relationship. Use emails to supplement rather than create in your social capital-building journey.

The best way to use emails while networking is to ask for one-on-one live meeting appointments. Once you have a name in mind with whom you would like to build a connection, drop them an email, speaking briefly about your scenario and asking for their time. Most business leaders and entrepreneurs receive hundreds of emails, so make sure you are able to fit into their time schedule. This means your message should be short and direct. Avoid long stories and too much background information in your email, and get to the point quickly. A total of four or five sentences should be good enough to convey your thoughts. The lengthier your email, the lower will be your chances of receiving a response. The best way to get a response is to ask for information. It is true that the purpose of networking is to find opportunities, but don't make the mistake of stating this in your email. Such points should be a part of a discussion rather than the start of a conversation. You are less likely to get an answer if all you have written in your email is "I'm looking for an opportunity to do XYZ, could you please help me with this by doing ABC?" Most people enjoy telling their own stories and there is nothing wrong with it, but reserve it for the live meeting.

2. DON'T SHY AWAY FROM ASKING FOR ACTION

Most people you will come across as you go about networking are kind enough to want to help you. It is, however, important that you are explicit about what you want from them. You don't want to bombard them with your list of wants right at the start, but be sure to communicate them in a good way at the appropriate time. In the fast-paced world we live in, everybody is so consumed by their own daily affairs that nobody has the time to think about what you need from them. If you feel that you sound pushy, you can soften your approach by using polite phrases such as "Would you be comfortable helping me with XYZ?" Many people also keep away from asking because of the fear of rejection. It is quite understandable to feel this way but you should remember that if one person says "No," that isn't the end of the world. There are many more people in the world who will be willing and able to help you. So, keep the faith and go on trying until you find the right connection for your particular business situation.

Another course of action many entrepreneurs fail to take is "follow up." Have you ever found yourself in a situation in which somebody promised to introduce you to another person, and a week went by with no response from them? If yes, what did you do in a circumstance like that? Most people would say they wanted to follow up but were either awkward or uncomfortable to do so. Such a reaction always results in lost opportunities, and would only make you feel dejected and pessimistic. So, whenever you have a meeting with any of your social contacts, always discuss the next steps with them then and there. For example, if someone told you they would introduce you to the CEO of a popular tech start-up in your city, you could say something like, "Thank you very much. I feel Joseph could be a useful person for me to get to know. How would you like to take this forward? Do you want me to contact Joseph directly and use you as a reference? Or would you prefer to speak to Joseph first and then introduce me to him? In case you would like to speak with him first, I will contact you next Wednesday to check on how your chat with Joseph went. Is that alright?" This way, both you and the other person will be on the same page with each knowing what to do. It also ensures that there's no room for any kind of awkwardness, misinterpretation, or interruption from either side.

3. YOU DON'T HAVE A WELL-CONSTRUCTED, UNIQUE SELLING PROPOSITION (USP)

Your USP is what sets you apart from the crowd, and is critical to your success as an entrepreneur wanting to build their social capital. You might be doing an amazing job with your business, but it's important for people to understand what you do in order for them to be able to help you. No matter how many networking events you attend and how many top-class business leaders you meet, all of it will have no meaning if they do not understand what you do and how you can add value to the lives of others. If you are looking for referrals from your social network, pick up a notepad and create that winning pitch for yourself and your business. The catchier your USP, the farther it will take you. It's not just about what you write to market yourself, it's also about how you present it. Passing on an improperly crafted USP in an ineffective manner is the greatest mistake most business people make. Your USP should include two elements, your target market, and how your product or service helps them. For example, your USP could be something like, "I help new lawyers market their services throughout the city in 60 days." Such a statement is sure to attract upcoming lawyers, and most of them will have follow-up questions for you to know more about how you can do this for them. Your goal with your USP should be to attract interest and capture the attention of your listeners, i.e., the people you meet at social events. This interest will then translate into further discussion, and probably more interactions and a strong relationship with the person in question.

4. DON'T USE THE COLD CALLING APPROACH

Both networking and cold calling involve interacting with people. It is important to remember that both these approaches are not the same. Cold calling is a quantitative approach that focuses on making as many calls as possible during a given period of time. Networking, on the other hand, is about relationships. The quality of the relationships you form is more important than the number. A person attending a social event with a cold calling approach would want to have short conversations with people and collect as many business cards as possible. Someone interested in building their social capital would spend their time having meaningful conversations with a few people and working to build those relationships with the aim of taking them to the next level at some point in the future. It entails getting to know people, asking good questions, and trying to evaluate how you can help one another. If you find yourself trying to talk to all the people at an event without focusing on relationship building, it's time you re-evaluate your approach. Face-to-face cold calling, as it is referred to, is in essence a waste of time and resources for you if you seriously want to build your social capital. In a bid to avoid cold calling, you shouldn't fall on the opposite end of the spectrum. This is where entrepreneurs tend to only interact with the people they know at every event they attend. Building relationships is not about spending all your time with the same people. You have to mix it up, whilst also keeping the balance. Speaking to the same people wherever you go will stagnate your social circle and stop your growth as an entrepreneur. Reflecting on your experience after every networking event is a helpful exercise. You can be aware of who you tend to engage with and how you spend your time. This exercise of periodically analyzing yourself will help you ward off unproductive behavioral patterns and inculcate helpful behaviors.

5. AVOID DELAYS & ABUSE

You work hard to attend networking events and create relationships with people you don't know only to get that referral for your business, and what happens when you get one? Ideally, if you receive the name and contact number of a social connection who would be interested in your business, the first and foremost thing you should be doing is to give them a call. This is unfortunately not what most entrepreneurs do. For some reason, they fail to respond immediately and end up losing the opportunity. Isn't this like wasting your own efforts? When you delay your response to a referral, it reflects unprofessionalism and disinterest on your end. Imagine how the other party would feel. Someone worked hard and took the initiative to send business your way, and you decided to respond leisurely after a week. The other person you were being introduced to will feel even more miserable and disrespected because they would have been informed that you would be calling them. So, no matter how busy your schedule is, always prioritize the job of responding to referrals. Most people don't have any good reason to explain this behavior. It is usually a result of forgetfulness or carelessness. All you have to do is make a call that will last three minutes or less, so attempt to do it almost immediately. Always treat your networking partners as your best clients. Returning their calls in time and responding to their interest in connecting with you promptly is a sign of your credibility as a business professional.

Abusing and misleading your connections is another strict no-no in networking. Let me tell you a story to explain this better. Daisy, an investment banker, had a long-standing working relationship of a year and a half with Henry. Their informal arrangement had ended about eight months before, and the two of them hadn't met since then. One winter Sunday, Daisy received an invitation card from Henry. It was for his 40th birthday party. Daisy really respected him and for the sake of the relationship they had shared, she decided she would attend the party. The day arrived and Daisy dressed in a casual party outfit, got a birthday present for Henry, and reached the venue at the time that was mentioned in the card. When she opened the door of the hall, she was surprised to see the people there. There was no music, no birthday decoration, and no sign of a party. A group of about 10 or 15 entrepreneurs, most of whom she could recognize, were seated in a semicircle in front of a projector. A middle-aged man, who was Henry's social contact, was presenting something, and Daisy discovered that this event had been organized to help this man raise money for his startup. Since she showed up, she had to join the event and was forced to sit there for an hour. This was supposed to be a birthday party with dinner, and all that was served to the guests was a milkshake. Daisy really felt disappointed, and this event affected her relationship with Henry in a negative way.

Trust is the most important ingredient of a networking relationship. It takes very long to build, and even longer to rebuild once it is broken. You must respect every one of your social connections. Just because you know somebody, it doesn't mean you can misuse that power for your own personal benefit. Doing so is a fatal mistake that many people, unfortunately, make as they go about building their social capital, so do everything you can to avoid it. Inviting somebody for a birthday party that turns out to be a business opportunity is in no way an honest and sincere networking effort.

6. DON'T WAIT FOR YOUR MIDLIFE CRISIS TO START NETWORKING

Networking is not a game of instant gratification like those you would find in a casino. If you start doing it today, you will rarely see results immediately. It is always advised that you should begin working on building your social capital as early as you can in your career. Many people often only take up this activity when they are going through a low phase or some kind of problem in their lives with the hope of finding a solution or opportunity. Such people always end up disappointed because nobody would want to help you unless they trust you, and trust cannot be built overnight. The best time to start networking is when you start thinking about your career. Do it at university, do it at work, and do it wherever you go. Even if you don't have a well-thought-out career plan in mind or you are a late bloomer unsure about what to do, your social capital is an asset you will be creating for yourself for your entire lifetime. If life's demands have been stopping you or you have been waiting for the right time to start, don't because that moment is now.

7. DON'T GO UNPREPARED

Whether you are attending your first ever networking event or have done it several times in the past, preparing for it is a step you should not skip. So what should your preparation comprise? Let's begin with the basics. First and foremost, think about what you will wear to the event and how you will get there. No matter how familiar you are with the city you live in, the venue you have to travel to, or the task of choosing an outfit for a networking event, you should start thinking about these things at least a day or two in advance. This will ensure that you have ample time to tackle issues like changing the way your outfit fits you, transportation strikes, or car problems. The second point to think about would be your objective for attending the event. Do you have a particular reason in mind or you would just like to generally socialize? While some people have the goal of getting referrals, others might be on the lookout for a mentor to receive guidance for their careers. Whatever it is that you want to do, make sure you think about it beforehand and be clear about how you will take it forward at the event. Organizing your thoughts in your head would be greatly beneficial, and will help keep nerves at ease. When you start talking to people, you will have to hold up the other end of the conversation, and if you do not know what you want from the event you are attending, you will be unable to do so. Many people think they have a fair idea of what they want, but they don't actually do, so take the time to know your purpose before every social event.

The third aspect that requires preparation is your pitch. Once you have a catchy well-written pitch ready for the event, keep practicing it until it comes naturally to you. Record yourself reading your pitch and listen to it. Repeat this activity a few times to monitor your progress. When you reach a level of perfection where your delivery no longer feels like a set of memorized lines being spoken aloud, you are good to go.

Finally, do not forget to carry your business cards along. Reaching out for your business card in your wallet and not finding it could be the most embarrassing moment for any entrepreneur, especially when you have someone you really want to give it to. You desperately want to build a connection with that person, but you don't have a business card to exchange. This little mistake can cost you enormously and can cause you to lose so many exciting opportunities. Imagine for a moment that you are at a wine and cheese party, and you meet an entrepreneur who doesn't have his business card and is fumbling to find tissue paper to write down his details for you. What will be your impression of him? Not favorable, right? So, think carefully about what you want to carry to the event, and get everything ready in time. Apart from an adequate number of business cards, you may need your pen, your reading glasses, your wallet with your credit card and cash, and some makeup if you're a woman. Going to an event unprepared causes unnecessary problems, and you will not be able to bring out the best in yourself and concentrate on what's truly important.

Another point worth mentioning here is concerned with your email address. When you're meeting somebody for the first time, email would most likely be your preferred means of communication with them. It is one of the most important components of your business card. It is therefore important that you have a decent professional-sounding email address. When we are younger, we tend to create funny email addresses for ourselves like bluepapaya@gmail.com. This might be cool for that age, but it surely isn't when you want to write an email to the managing director of a venture capital company or the co-founder of a multi-million dollar business. The best email address you can have for yourself is one containing your full name. For example, johnclark@xyz.com. You could add punctuations to this or probably numbers if the exact name isn't available, but having your name in your email address is important. It shows you are serious about what you're doing.

8. DON'T WASTE TIME WITH UNHELPFUL CONVERSATIONS

Networking is all about conversations. You should try to make good use of your time at every event you attend. You will meet people who like to only talk about business, but you will also come across some who like to go on and on about everything in the world. Your goal should be to derive as much value from the event as you can, and whether or not you are able to achieve this will depend upon the kind of people you spend most of your time with. If you feel the conversation is moving off-topic, try to bring it back by shifting the topic to something useful. Don't wait for the other person to do this for you. If you aren't able to refocus the discussion, let the person complete their point and politely excuse yourself once they are done. Don't make the ending abrupt though. Say a sentence or two to conclude before you leave the place. Many people tend to feel uncomfortable closing a conversation or even changing the topic. There is absolutely no need to feel this way. Whom you wish to speak to and for how long should entirely be your call. Be polite and respect the person you are conversing with, and everything will go well for you.

9. DON'T TALK WITH YOUR MOUTH FULL

We all love food, and it also gives us comfort during anxious moments, but talking in the middle of a bite is a sign of disrespect. It shows you have no manners. It might also sometimes come across as if you are too busy eating and aren't paying attention to what the other person is saying. Even if you are meeting someone over dinner, give more importance to talking than eating. If you need to eat, munch gently and keep the meal small. According to science, the human brain is not designed to multitask. So listen actively and make sure speaking is your primary activity. Another eating-related habit that leaves a not-so-favorable impression on others is chewing gum. Continuously munching on gum and doing so in a noisy and obvious way when in a conversation with someone can make you appear unprofessional and also distract them. In order to ensure that your speech is clear and you come across as a professional person who is interested in networking with the people around you, finish eating before you start talking. You cannot imagine how much of an impression little things like eating the wrong way and at the wrong time can make.

10. DON'T EVER MAKE A MISTAKE WITH NAMES

When you attend a social event, you will meet people of different cultural backgrounds and ethnicities. These people may have names you are not familiar with. This is quite a normal situation that happens with almost everyone, but if you know how to handle it, this will most likely not cause any kind of problem for you in your networking journey. If you know who you're going to meet and if the interaction is preplanned, take the time to go through the name of the person and try to figure out how to pronounce it correctly. You could ask a friend to help you with your pronunciation or else just research it online. Not saying someone's name the right way can really make them feel offended and can sometimes even hurt their feelings. There will however be situations when you do not have the time to practice or research. The best thing to do in such a circumstance is to ask the person if you are pronouncing their name correctly or not. In the unfortunate situation that you end up making a mistake with your pronunciation, quickly apologize and be honest. Don't make fun of the name or say that it is difficult to pronounce. Respect it and compliment it instead. If you have a bad memory, confess that to your contact rather than making some other excuse. One trick that you can use to help tackle the name problem is this. As soon as you meet someone and once the initial introduction is over, say, "Great to meet you, Name!" Try to repeat the name at the end or the beginning of a few other remarks or comments after that. For example: "So Veena, what's your new venture all about?" or "I like your idea, Xian.". This will help cement the name in your mind and reduce the chances of errors such as mispronunciation or using the wrong name.

11. WATCH YOUR TALKING

There are a few mistakes people tend to make in this regard. The first one is talking too much. Everyone likes a good conversation and the fact that you are talking makes the other person feel that you are having a good time. People however want to be heard as much as they like listening. A conversation is supposed to be a two-way street. When you allow people to talk, they tend to feel important and valued. So, be mindful about how much you speak in a conversation, and give the other person enough space to express their opinion. Don't make the mistake of saying too little, though. In the process of trying to give the opposite person a chance to talk, many people end up speaking too little. Achieving the right balance is not very difficult. Just concentrate all your attention on that conversation, be consciously aware of what you are doing, and try to be your natural self. The basic rule of thumb is to listen twice as much as you talk. Always remember that you are at an event to network, not to deliver a monologue or a sale pitch. Allowing people to talk will give you an opportunity to understand them and figure out how the two of you could work with one another.

Another common mistake many business people tend to make is rushing through a conversation in order to get to the next one. Networking is definitely not about speaking to just one person, but it is important that you give your 100% to every conversation you are a part of. Most people want to cover as many attendees as possible at an event, and this is what leads them to make mistakes such as speaking too fast, too little, or just talking in haste. Rushing through conversations will have no meaning and will absolutely bring you no value. You won't be able to concentrate or remember your conversations. Wanting to meet and interact with as many people as possible at a social event isn't wrong, but don't do it at the cost of compromising on the quality of your conversations.

12. DON'T PREJUDGE PEOPLE

We all know the popular phrase, "Don't judge a book by its cover," but we still do it. We don't just do it with books, but we also end up doing it with people. It is humanly impossible to predict what a person is capable of without speaking to them and getting to know them closely. Many physical attributes such as shyness, a bad posture, and sometimes even odd facial features or body structure put us off and prevent us from socializing with people. The first thing to remember here is that many physical aspects of a person's personality are not within their control. You don't control your height, your facial features, the color of your skin, or the texture of your hair. You are born with them. So, don't judge people on the basis of these attributes. If you just take a moment to go down the annals of history, you will find success stories, billionaires, corporate giants, and genius minds in every nook and corner of the globe, in every culture and every nationality. You should, therefore, make a decision about people on the basis of conversations and achievements. When you look at a person and spend time with them, you're likely to fall victim to stereotypes, but don't let them rule your decisions. Whether you are getting into a relationship with a person or choosing to dismiss them, always do it with an ample amount of forethought and a calm mind. Many people also tend to judge others on the basis of how they speak during the first meeting. Everyone wants to make the best first impression, and all the people you meet have surely prepared themselves to do so, but things can go wrong. It is human to make mistakes. Everything that happens within us and around us isn't entirely in our control. What you are going through in your personal life, for example, will also have an impact on your behavior and performance at networking events, and it is the same for everyone you meet. So give time to a relationship and to the people you meet before you jump to any sort of conclusion about them.

13. DON'T RESTRICT YOURSELF

Networking has some rules and best practices, but no boundaries. The benefits that come from building your social capital are not limited to one kind of networking or one particular social organization. No matter where you come from, you have the freedom to socialize with the kind of people you want to and in the way you like to. The goal is to build connections, so it doesn't necessarily have to happen through a world-class networking organization. You also shouldn't limit yourself to one industry or region. Try to connect with people from different ethnic groups, cultural backgrounds, nationalities, age groups, genders, and income levels. If you are a female working in the financial sector in London, you may restrict yourself to networking groups targeted only at women, finance professionals, or Londoners. This isn't always done consciously, but that's how it works for most people. Many of us also find it awkward to mingle with people outside our own income bracket. We feel uncomfortable meeting those who are wealthier and don't value those who fall below our level as much. It cannot be stressed enough that every person is important and useful in some way. So break all boundaries and network with all kinds of people.

14. DON'T MAKE THESE VIRTUAL NETWORKING MISTAKES

Whether you like it or not, and whether you are comfortable with it or not, Zoom calls and Skype meetings are commonplace today. It might not be the primary method of networking, but it is certainly a part of every person's socializing approach. It is, therefore, important to be aware of the rights and wrongs of virtual networking as well. So what are some of the mistakes you can avoid when attending online meetings and events?

- Don't focus only on building new connections. Quantity is not more important than quality. When we look at the profiles of so many entrepreneurs and business leaders, we oftentimes get tempted to add them to our network but do not always have the time to build those relationships. So take it slowly.

- Never send LinkedIn invitations without a personal message. Even one or two sentences specifically written for the person you want to connect with can make a huge difference, and more so if you have never met them before. Which of the following sounds better for an invitation request on the social media site? "Join my network on LinkedIn," or, "Hi Jack. Remember me? We used to work together five years ago. I'd love to catch up with you. Please add me and let's see when we can meet for coffee." If you were to receive an invitation request from someone on LinkedIn, wouldn't you like the second option better?

- Don't place your focus only on connecting with high-level contacts. It's good to make a relationship with people who have more experience than you, but forming lateral connections could also be equally beneficial. The people who are sailing in the same boat as you will be able to share so much with you and all of that knowledge can greatly help you in advancing your career.

- Consider accessibility before planning a virtual meeting. Not everyone is equal in terms of their abilities. There are a number of people out there who suffer from disabilities of different kinds and might have special needs when attending an online session. For example, the deaf will require sign language experts and the partially sighted will need voice interpretation for the visual aspects of the event. So, be mindful and aware of the needs of everyone you network with, and especially sensitive to those of the differently abled. Navigating an event or meeting on an online platform is many times more difficult than doing it offline for some people. Try to be helpful, and do whatever you can to make them feel comfortable without hurting their feelings.

- Avoid having an unprofessional setup for your virtual meeting. You might be at home in your room, but your workspace speaks a lot about you. A messy background such as piled up laundry, undone dishes, cushions and pillows all over the place, a bed that is not made, and an untidy room overall is not the best sight to look at for anyone. Make sure to clean your space before you join the event. Adjust your microphone and camera well in time for the event to avoid embarrassing scenes such as a zoomed-in focus on your nose hair or face. Do not make the mistake of ignoring your workplace and not testing your video, audio, and connectivity before every networking event you attend online.

- Dress up for an online event in the same way as you would for a face-to-face one. Avoid slipping into pajamas and thinking that it will go unnoticed. An image of even a part of your clothing can give the opposite person a fair idea of what you are wearing. You must also ensure that your hair and face look nice and presentable because your facial expression is what will be the most visible part of you to your viewers. It's very important to make a good impression at a social networking event, and since your body language is not going to be visible and what you speak is only going to account for a small part of your overall personality, your face, clothes, and background need to be given prime importance. Virtual networking is not very different from its traditional counterpart, so many of the rules and tips we have discussed earlier in the book apply here as well.

15. DON'T GIVE UP

Hard work and persistence are two of the prerequisites for success in networking. Keeping your patience is very important as well. Entrepreneurs who step back and give up normally do so after one unsuccessful attempt. The enormity of the job also causes many people to withdraw even before trying. Failure is a part of life. Where there is work, there will be success and there will be failure too. You will never be able to know what you are capable of unless you try. Don't be daunted. You have within you everything it takes to become mighty successful at networking. Knowledge is power, and you have absorbed a lot of it as you flipped through the pages of this book. So feel confident about your abilities, and don't let failure or fear pull you back. Here is a little story to motivate you.

Long long ago, when the world was a much smaller place, there lived a merchant in a beautiful seaside town. He was wealthy and famous. A large state-of-the-art ship was one of his most valuable possessions. One summer afternoon, he decided to go on a voyage on his ship. Preparations began, and a hundred servants from his massive workforce were rushing back and forth to ensure everything was set for the journey. Just when the ship was about to depart, they discovered that the engine wouldn't start. Mechanics were called to check it, but they could do nothing. The best engineers in town spent days together to fix the machine, but none of their efforts bore fruit. Since nobody seemed to have a solution to this problem, the merchant decided to call an engineer from the neighboring town. This engineer was a very old man and promptly arrived at the mansion to help the merchant. The merchant explained the problem to him, and his servants escorted him to the ship. The old engineer had a large bag of tools with him, but he didn't pull out a single one from it. He began looking at the engine from different directions and angles. The merchant and his servants looked at one another and thought that this was going to be another failed attempt. After examining the engine for about ten minutes, the old engineer pulled out a hammer and hit the machine in a particular spot. He did it once, and after a few moments, he did it again. Much to the surprise of all the witnesses, the engine started working. The merchant was elated.

The next morning, the servants at the mansion received a bill from the old engineer for $10,000. Finding this figure to be too high, the merchant immediately called the engineer. "You only worked on the ship for about 15 minutes and used nothing other than a hammer, so what is this bill all about?" the merchant asked.

"It's one dollar for using the hammer and $9,999 to know how and where to use it."

The merchant was amazed. He was overflowing with respect for the engineer and paid him more than what he had asked for. This was just a little story, but it can become the reality of your life. Knowledge has the power to bring you enormous success if you don't give up and keep trying.

So these were some of the most common mistakes you must avoid when you go out to network. No list can be exhaustive. Every individual in the world is different, and the way they react and respond to circumstances will also be. Your journey will therefore never be exactly the same as someone else's. Embrace your unique story, and don't let your mistakes discourage you or pull you back. Embarrassments are normal, don't take them to heart. They happen to the best of us. Do you remember how many times you fell before you learned to walk perfectly? The number would have been high for sure, but what's more important is that you kept trying and finally succeeded. Recreate this success story in your networking journey, make those mistakes and let your own experience be your greatest teacher.

FINAL WORDS

You have now reached the end of the social capital saga. Let's quickly recap what we did so far. Our journey together began with a discussion about the three types of capital, financial capital, human capital, and social capital.

- Financial capital is all about tangible stuff, i.e., money. When people say capital, they usually mean financial capital. We needed it in every aspect of our business right from incorporation to winding up.

- Human capital is the second type of capital we discussed and is about intangible stuff. It has to do with the training we provide to our employees, the skills they bring to our business, the previous work experience they have, and so on.

- The third and final type of capital is the one this entire book was all about, i.e., social capital. In simple words, social capital is business networking. The explanation of the term also included a description of the three types of social capital, bonding capital (networking within a single group or community), bridging capital (socializing with people from different groups), and linking capital (building relationships with people of a higher status and income level).

The discussion then progressed to the benefits of building your social capital. One point that sums this section up in the best and most concise way is, "No man is an island." Nobody in the world can accomplish everything all by themselves. Neither were the greatest inventors of the past able to do it, nor will anybody in the future. We need people for advice and guidance, to answer many of our unanswered questions, and to help us in fulfilling our entrepreneurial dreams. These people will be willing to help us only if we build a good relationship with them. Networking can help us create these relationships.

Research shows that any person in the world is only six connections away from you. So, you can basically get to any person you want in the world and build a relationship with them if you network the right way. In the following chapter, we learned about the different ways in which you can build your social capital and bring this goldmine into your life. Failing to plan is like planning to fail, and this principle applies to networking as well. The chapter also included information about how to plan your networking journey, how to monitor your progress, and how to reach the peak of success.

As you flipped through the pages, you discovered the various benefits that building your social capital can bring into your life. Why should I work towards accumulating social capital? How is this asset going to help me in my career? Will building my social capital improve my physical and mental health? This chapter contained answers to these and many more such questions.

Meeting people and interacting with them is only the start. You can only expect to gain from them if you put in the effort to maintain them. When you form a new relationship, don't forget the old ones. Building and maintaining relationships should be a permanent part of your life. We discussed the different methods you can use to maintain your relationships.

Life is too fast-paced for everyone these days, and for someone who is running a business, there is always a seemingly never-ending to-do list to fulfill. People want to network, but they do not have the time to research which organizations they should join. We made your job easier in the following chapter. We introduced you to some of the most popular networking organizations out there, and the list can come in handy whenever you are in the mood to join one.

When entrepreneurs try to strike a chord with successful business people in the corporate world, the ultimate aim is to make a profit. Mingling with people and getting introduced to new ones is a good thing, but earning a real buck from a relationship requires a business alliance. Read any business journal or newspaper, and you will find information about alliances of large businesses every so often. These partnerships are the ultimate result of that first handshake you extended your hand to someone at a wine and cheese party, for example. In the chapter on business alliances, we discussed:

- What is a business alliance?

- What are the different ways in which you can form a business alliance with someone?

- Details about the three types of business alliances.

- How can a business alliance benefit you?

- Some tips and tricks to ensure your alliance is successful

Attending social events, exchanging pleasantries with people, starting conversations, introducing oneself, and the various other aspects of socializing do not come naturally to everyone. Everyone has the ability to attain success at networking, but most people aren't born with everything that is required to get there. While some personality traits can help you in your journey, there are certain behaviors that can slow your progress. This chapter will provide you with a good understanding of what those beneficial skills are, and how you can inculcate and use them when you go about building your social capital. Here are some of the aspects we covered:

- How to dress up for a networking event.

- How to manage social anxiety.

- How to impress the people you meet.

- How to talk and what to say.

- Everything you need to know to prepare yourself for socialization.

The final chapter was all about looking at networking from another lens. In the first seven chapters of the book, we learned about all the rules and the right things to do, and in this final one, we discussed the mistakes. It is not easy to spot and correct a mistake all by yourself. Not many people in the world will tell you where you are going wrong. It is true that every personality is different and so are the mistakes they can make, but there are some common ones that most people end up making. We have tried to cover as many of these as possible in this chapter. Keeping them in mind will get alarm bells ringing in your head when the scenario arises that you are on the brink of making that mistake.

There is a lot we have discussed about social capital all throughout this book, but it cannot be stressed enough that you must use this knowledge to create an approach that works for you. Take for instance that you love the design of a dress worn by a celebrity on the cover of Vogue, what would you do? Will you take the dress as it is and wear it or would you ask for it to be tailored to your size? I am sure you chose the second option. The same applies to networking as well. Equip yourself with all the knowledge from this book, but apply it to your life by using your own judgment.

Building your social capital requires hard work. Start as early as you can, add value to the lives of other people in whichever way you can without expecting anything in return, work to build the relationships you create, and keep trying until you succeed. The right combination of knowledge and hard work can help you conquer the stars and transform your life for the better.

"You can make more friends in two months by becoming interested in other people than you can in two years by trying to get other people interested in you." - Dale Carnegie

"The richest people in the world look for and build networks, everyone else looks for work. Marinate on that for a minute." - Robert Kiyosaki

If you enjoyed reading this book and found the content informative, please consider leaving us a review on Amazon. And if you are in the mood to apply the freshly learned principles of networking, you could even add value to the lives of your connections by sharing this book with them.

REFERENCES
······················

Kirsch, Katrina. 2021. "18 Networks All Entrepreneurs Should Consider Joining". HubSpot. https://blog.hubspot.com/sales/entrepreneur-networks (accessed: 01/09/2022)

Thweatt, Dyllan. 2022. "20 Best Quotes About Networking And How To Act On Them". Affinity. https://www.affinity.co/blog/quotes-networking?hs_amp=true (accessed: 02/09/2022)

Insureon 2022. "The 10 Best Small Business Networking Groups". Insureon. https://www.insureon.com/blog/best-small-business-groups-for-networking (accessed: 25/08/2022)

Misner, Ivan. 2022. "The 5 Types Of Business Networking Organizations". Entrepreneur. https://www.entrepreneur.com/article/302630 (accessed: 25/08/2022)

Woog, Dan. 2022. "13 Networking Mistakes". Monster. https://www.monster.com/career-advice/article/thirteen-networking-mistakes (accessed: 01/09/2022)

Huggett, Jill. 2020. "How To Avoid 6 Common Networking Mistakes". Forbes. https://www.forbes.com/sites/forbescoachescouncil/2020/01/10/how-to-avoid-six-common-networking-mistakes/?sh=64896a742e1d (accessed: 29/08/2022)

Hilliard, Brian. 2022. "5 Most Common Networking Mistakes". Entrepreneur. https://www.entrepreneur.com/article/302633 (accessed: 15/08/2022)

Landers contributor 2019. "10 Do's And Don'ts Of Networking". Ladders. https://www.theladders.com/career-advice/10-dos-and-donts-of-networking/amp (accessed: 30/08/2022)

Indeed Editorial Team 2021. "Top 7 Networking Skills - How To Develop And Highlight Them". Indeed. https://in.indeed.com/career-advice/career-development/networking-skills (accessed: 22/08/2022)

Adams, R.L. 2022. "10 Powerful Networking Skills To Build Rapport Quickly". Entrepreneur. https://www.entrepreneur.com/article/301087 (accessed: 27/08/2022)

Wikipedia 2022. "Financial Capital". Wikipedia. https://en.m.wikipedia.org/wiki/Financial_capital (accessed: 19/05/2022)

Kenton, Will. 2021. "What Is Social Capital". Investopedia. https://www.investopedia.com/terms/s/socialcapital.asp (accessed: 24/05/2022)

Wikipedia 2022. "Social Capital". Wikipedia. https://en.m.wikipedia.org/wiki/Social_capital (accessed: 30/06/2022)

Kenton, Will. 2022. "Human Capital". Investopedia. https://www.investopedia.com/terms/h/humancapital.asp (accessed: 20/05/2022)

Young, Janette. 2012. "Social Capital Theory - An Overview". Science Direct. https://www.sciencedirect.com/topics/social-sciences/social-capital-theory (accessed: 03/06/2022)

Cancialosi, Chris. 2022. "4 Reasons Why Social Capital Trumps All". Forbes. https://www.forbes.com/sites/chriscancialosi/2014/09/22/4-reasons-social-capital-trumps-all/amp/ (accessed: 26/06/2022)

Marcus, Bonnie. 2022. "Your Network Is Your Net Worth: 7 Ways To Build Social Capital". Forbes. https://www.forbes.com/sites/bonniemarcus/2014/10/20/your-network-is-your-net-worth-7-ways-to-build-social-capital/?sh=f0c9e246af77 (accessed: 01/07/2022)

Claridge, Tristan. 2021. "How Do You Increase Your Social Capital". Social Capital Research. https://www.socialcapitalresearch.com/how-do-you-increase-your-social-capital/amp/ (accessed: 10/07/2022)

Webb, Liggy. 2013. "8 Tips For Developing Positive Relationships". Training Mag. https://trainingmag.com/8-tips-for-developing-positive-relationships/ (accessed: 15/07/2022)

Forbes Business Council 2022. "How To Build Authentic Business Relationships". Forbes. https://www.forbes.com/sites/forbesbusiness-council/2021/06/15/how-to-build-authentic-business-relationships/amp/ (accessed: 20/07/2022)

Corporate Finance Institute 2022. "Strategic Alliances". Corporate Finance Institute. https://corporatefinanceinstitute.com/resources/knowledge/strategy/strategic-alliances/ (accessed: 20/07/2022)

Huhn, Jessica. 2022. "10 Strategic Alliance Examples And What You Can Learn From Them". Referral Rock. https://referralrock.com/blog/strategic-alliance-examples/ (accessed: 15/08/2022)

Wikipedia 2022. "Six Degrees Of Separation Theory". Wikipedia. https://en.wikipedia.org/wiki/Six_degrees_of_separation#:~:text=Six%20degrees%20of%20separation%20is,as%20the%20six%20handshakes%20rule. (Accessed:18/09/2022)

Forbes 2022. "Profile Elon Musk". Forbes. https://www.forbes.com/profile/elon-musk/?list=rtb/&sh=2eec04c17999 (Accessed: 18/09/2022)

ABOUT AUTHOR

MICHAEL WILSON is a business coach turned author from McAllen, Texas, whose book The Millionaires' Secret focuses on building networks to improve business. Several years ago, Michael recognized a noticeable lack of prioritization of networking. Applying concepts he learned from his business coaching practice, Michael seized on the opportunity and embarked on his journey to coach business owners on the value of building their sphere of influence. His mantra is "Your Net Worth is Your Network"

Today Michael is a certified John Maxwell Coach. He has attained an Associate degree in Business Management, a bachelor's in technology management, an MBA, and has been accepted for a Doctoral in Strategic Leadership. A Network Lead Exchange chapter owner and the co-owner of Entrepreneur Power Network and FocusedForward Business Coaching, he works with companies all over the U.S. developing growth strategies, one benchmark at a time, until the final, most significant target is secured.

FOLLOW ME

FACEBOOK

facebook.com/michaeljpwilson

LINKEDIN

linkedin.com/in/mmwilson1274

YOUTUBE

Powerful Business Resources and Tools

www.entrepreneurpowernetwork.com

JOIN A CHAPTER NEAR YOU

Network Lead Exchange provides the opportunity to build your social capital (network) fast.

Join a local chapter near you

Tell them that Michael Wilson Referred You

www.networkleadexchange.com

The Future Of Networking

SPEAKING OR WORKSHOP

Do you have an event that needs a speaker or workshop facilitator on the topic of building business networks or spheres of influence? Michael Wilson has extensive experience in helping people build their networks. His powerful workshop will have participants dominating future networking events.

MEET OUR MEMBERS

Joe Martinez, Big Joe Supreme Credit Services
Tessa Coral, New York Life
Anthony Perez, Bold Insurance
Austin Imports Tea and Honey
Richard Gomez, Rebel Leads
Rosalinda Villa, Angel Wings Carriers
Carlos Diaz, Virtual Business Office
Carmen Pedraza Silva, United Enterprises
Moises Segovia, Life Starr EMS
Heather Segovia, St. Michaels Ambulance
Nikki Falcon, Prosperity Health Care
Denise Orton, Denise's Wellness
Felipe Saavedra, Building Quality Homes
Carlos Garcia, Family Life Concepts
Celeste Huff, Texas Consulting Agency
Get More Info About Their Business Below